Love Is Stronger Than Death

Rick Rotondi

www.cenacle.tv

Copyright © 2024 by Rick Rotondi

All rights reserved.

No portion of this book may be reproduced in any form without written permission from the publisher or author, except as permitted by U.S. copyright law.

Excerpt from *Roy Schoeman's Conversion Story* © Roy Schoeman. Used with permission.

Cover image (Vilnius Divine Mercy image) and sections "How to Pray the Divine Mercy Chaplet" and "How to Pray the Divine Mercy Novena" used with permission of the Marian Fathers of the Immaculate Conception of the Blessed Virgin Mary. Stockbridge, MA USA.

Interior photos and images are © Rick Rotondi, © Melanie Rotondi, and from public domain and licensed stock image sources.

Book cover and interior design by Melanie Rotondi.

Published by Cenacle, York, SC.

First Edition

To those who mourn

"Blessed are they who mourn, for they shall be comforted."
— Matthew 5:4

Olivia Marie Rotondi
June 19, 1996 — May 5, 2022

Timeline

April 2, 2022

Rick and Melanie invited to begin
praying the Divine Mercy Chaplet for
a successful Holy Land Pilgrimage

April 24, 2022

Divine Mercy Sunday
Melanie and Rick obtain the Divine Mercy indulgence
and offer it to the Blessed Virgin Mary

May 1, 2022

Barbecue at Paradiso

May 4, 2022

Olivia checks into hotel

May 5, 2022

Prayer requests sent out for Olivia
Interior message received: *"I've got her!"*
Olivia found dead

May 6, 2022

Funeral planning
Rainbow over Paradiso

May 10, 2022

Olivia's Wake

May 11, 2022

Olivia's Funeral and Burial

May 12 – 13, 2022

Trip to Charleston for the Episcopal Ordination of
Bishop Jacques Fabre-Jeune

Contents

		X
1.	Phone Calls	1
2.	Foreboding	7
3.	Hotel	15
4.	Chasms	21
5.	Mercy	27
6.	I've Got Her!	41
7.	Angels	51
8.	Chapel	59
9.	Funeral	65
10.	Charleston	75
Epilogue		87
Endnotes		98
How to Pray the Divine Mercy Chaplet		101
How to Pray the Divine Mercy Novena		107
About the Author		127

This book is a true story. It reflects the author's recollection of events. Some names and locations have been changed to protect the privacy of those depicted. Dialogue has been re-created from memory.

1

Phone Calls

The day my daughter Olivia died I received a call from my son, Tim, at 7:03 a.m. Tim was concerned that Olivia had not come home the night before.

Since Olivia was on my cell phone plan, Tim asked me to check her call and text history and see if I could ping her location. That was a technological challenge for a 53-year-old father at 7:03 a.m. I opened my cell phone app and fumbled through it, seeing what I could find.

There wasn't much. I couldn't map her cell phone. I did see Olivia's phone and text history, but nothing stood out. There were no calls or texts from the previous evening, when she had left the Charlotte townhome where she lived with Tim and her mother. And there were none after.

At 7:21 a.m. Tim called again. "I'm not worried," I told him. "She probably went out with friends last night, stayed over, and is sleeping in."

Olivia had lived with me for a year or so before moving back to live with Tim and her mother. As a young twentysomething she'd stayed out before. I'd fretted through a few late nights unable to reach her. By late morning her jaunty white coupe would always roll in.

But as the minutes passed, and over several more texts and calls, I did worry.

Calls went out to Olivia's closest friends. They didn't know where Olivia was. Then we discovered an empty package for a food preservative was found in her room. Olivia enjoyed camping with friends; perhaps that was its purpose? A Google search, however, revealed a more disturbing use. The preservative is sometimes, and increasingly, used for suicide. Various internet forums discussed it openly.

At 7:32 a.m. I sent my own text to Olivia.

> *Hey Sweetie! How's it going? Are you OK? I got a call from Tim and Mom that they don't know where you are. Please give me a call! Love, Dad*

At 7:45 a.m. I called my wife, Melanie, already at work 50 minutes away in Uptown Charlotte. I asked Melanie to pray for Olivia. I saw no need for her to return.

At 8:01 a.m., I received a call from Conor Gallagher, CEO of TAN Books, my friend and former boss. A request for prayers for Olivia had been sent to several email distribution lists. Conor had been alerted. What was going on?

We discussed what I knew, and the typical pattern of missing person reports. I clung to reassuring facts. Olivia was almost 26 years old. She had headed out the evening before on her own and had been gone less than 12 hours. Most of these situations are resolved safely. She was likely sleeping in with friends after a late night.

Olivia's workday began at 9 a.m. I waited to learn if she had shown up for work. As the clock ticked forward, I paced back and forth, nervously anticipating a call.

A few moments before the 9 a.m. deadline, I grew strangely composed. I had a strong inner sense or impression that Olivia was OK. Perhaps it was simply shock, an instinctual mechanism to keep the potential magnitude of my loss from overwhelming my mind. No doubt that was an element.

But I also felt the comforting presence of the Lord. *I am with you always* (Mt 28:20), Jesus told the apostles before ascending into Heaven. Of course He was with me now.

And I believed He was with me not only as Lord but also as friend, Jesus' wonderful word for the apostles in His farewell discourse at the Last Supper. *I have called you friends* (Jn 15:15).

I wasn't an apostle, but I was bold enough to claim the term by extension. For 32 years, I had labored in the vineyard of Catholic publishing. However fumbling, I was a disciple. Therefore, I was His friend. I felt the assurance of it in my soul. I didn't hear Him speak to me. But I felt His presence, His power, His love, His promise that "all shall be well."[1] My mind shaped this into words:

> *Rick, I'm your friend. Of*
> *course I will take care of*

Olivia. I've got her.

I waited calmly for news. Shortly after 9 a.m. I learned that Olivia hadn't come to work.

The rest of the morning unfolded in a hailstorm of calls.

There was a conference call with two police officers who had come to make a report on Olivia. I grasped hungrily at their grounds for hope.

"We don't have evidence she's in immediate danger," one told us. "I know you have a concern about the packaging for the food preservative you found. You've researched it on the web and seen it tied to suicides. But your daughter would have to be a pharmacist to use it that way."

Then there was the organizing of a search. Friends and family fanned out over Charlotte, scouring parking lots for Olivia's distinctive white coupe.

Melanie was already on her way back to Paradiso, our small farmhouse in York, South Carolina. I had told Melanie about finding the sodium nitrate. She had also received a concerned call from a friend, Terry DeMao, who, like Conor, had received an emailed prayer request for Olivia. Melanie raced home filled with dread.

Before Melanie arrived I received another call. Olivia's car had been found in the parking lot of a hotel in Charlotte near where she lived.

"Is there anyone in the car?" I wondered. We didn't know.

Another call followed shortly. Olivia had checked into the hotel the evening before. Other family members and friends were now on site. The hotel wouldn't allow access to Olivia's room until the police arrived.

The crunch of gravel on Melanie's tires announced her arrival home. We embraced quickly in our driveway, then both took our seats. Melanie sped us towards the hotel as I fielded increasingly frantic calls.

I clung to the hope that Olivia would be OK; that we'd find her, a Sleeping Beauty, safe in her hotel room. I told Melanie of the profound peace I had been given earlier, the words *I've got her* seemingly a direct message from the Lord, pressed upon my soul.

The ground fell away forever with the next call. The police had gone into the hotel room. Olivia was dead.

Our hearts breaking, Melanie and I continued to the hotel, as I called my parents, sisters, and Uncle Stephen to break the news of Olivia's death.

Speed was the outlet for our agony. Melanie made the usual 50-minute drive in about half the time.

Rick's car next to Olivia's

2

FOREBODING

Olivia's death by suicide was an unimaginable shock. Other bereavements I had discerned from afar, steeling myself as they approached slowly and ominously. Olivia's death was different. It shredded my heart with the suddenness and viciousness of a terrorist attack or IED.

Just days before Olivia took her life, Melanie and I had spent hours with her, laughing, talking, and eating. On Sunday, May 1, we hosted an outdoor BBQ at Paradiso, smoke-grilling 14 racks of baby back ribs on our huge custom-made smoker and sharing them with Olivia, Tim, Tim's girlfriend, Elizabeth, and about 40 other guests. Family and friends had gathered to feast, enjoy rides in our farm cart, and play a few holes of what we call "farm golf." In the evening we had watched the sun set down by the lake, then gathered by the firepit as the stars winked on in the darkening sky.

Olivia was beautiful, happy and at ease — more so than I had seen her in a long time. The past year had brought challenges. She'd broken up with a boyfriend and taken a semester off from the Master of Counseling degree she was pursuing online. She'd resumed classes and completed her coursework in January but had not obtained a counseling internship. She'd taken a position at an insurance company instead. She seemed to enjoy the camaraderie of her new job and the opportunity to move from student to wage earner.

She'd made a confession when, seated around the fire pit, I asked her about work. "Sometimes I wish I could just work at Holy Angels," she'd said wistfully. Holy Angels was a residence in Belmont for persons with significant developmental disabilities. Olivia had been a caregiver there while studying for her master's degree. Her loving and protective nature suited her perfectly for the job. She bonded deeply with the residents, and they with her.

Olivia's warmth and sweetness were striking and genuine, her most salient qualities. But she could be angry, too, if she felt thwarted or pushed too hard to venture outside her comfort zone. In college, I had incurred her anger for not replacing a car I had provided after a flood took it. Her anger was long simmering, expressing itself in silence and avoidance of contact.

In the last year of her life, her anger towards me had diminished, but it had not disappeared.

Olivia's warmth also coexisted with sadness, a hesitancy towards life that became more apparent as she grew. I can't deny it. Occasionally, these facets of her personality would appear, like outcroppings of icebergs on otherwise placid seas. I knew they were dangerous, but I didn't realize the massive weight, depth, and shape of what lurked below.

My first iceberg sighting was when Olivia was in elementary school. She was, her teachers told me, a good student: smart, diligent, and respectful. And quiet; too quiet. She didn't speak up. She didn't actively participate. My heart sank as I heard her teacher's report, and as I saw its prescience over the years. Olivia shrank from social involvement. She deflected my clumsy encouragements to join extracurricular activities, get a job, even, later in life, go outside, mix and mingle, and not spend so much time in her room.

She loved relaxing, indoors and outdoors, and enjoying time with family. She had wonderful friends, with whom she enjoyed planning and engaging in fun activities, including concerts, beach trips, and hiking excursions. She also spent hours alone, listening to indie music or going online. She wasn't active on Facebook or social media where I was present. But she surprised me in middle school when she told me she had a Tumblr account. She left the main thoroughfares of the internet for less frequented byways and alleys.

How I wish I had been more aware of their dangers.

When Olivia was a child I could protect her. I often recall the day when Olivia, just three years old, swallowed a quarter as I watched her at home. She came to me, tugged my hand, and pointed at her throat, unable to speak, unable to breathe, unable to dislodge the obstruction inside. I turned her around and performed the Heimlich maneuver. Up came the quarter. I hugged her close, cried in relief, and thanked God that the danger of suffocation had been averted.

O my daughter Olivia, my daughter, my daughter Olivia! Why was I unable to get up the deeper obstruction inside you, your sadness, your anxiety, your feeling of brokenness? Why could I not perform a Heimlich maneuver for your soul?

Olivia had a loving family. We doted on her: An only daughter and, on my side of the family, an only granddaughter. Despite this special status, Olivia was also part of a large extended family with many beloved cousins, including Siena and Sophia, second cousins who were close in age. Some of Olivia's most treasured memories were her summer vacations with Papa and Grandma Rotondi, cousins Quinn and Cole, and other family in Wolfeboro, New Hampshire.

Olivia's childhood also had its sorrows. I became a single dad when Olivia was three years old. Thereafter I exercised my fatherhood through phone calls, afternoon outings, school and sports events, weekend visits, and family vacations.

The breaking of our household was a bereavement, a harbinger of the bereavement to come. I grieved not providing Olivia and Tim the great blessing of my own childhood, an intact family. I was grateful the separation and divorce happened in their early years, before most of their memories formed.

I wanted to be available for Olivia and Tim as best I could. I settled into the life of a single father and confirmed bachelor, a status I kept until Olivia and Tim had finished school. Once they had grown, God brought Melanie into my life in a most beautiful way. After a 15-month courtship we married in 2021.

We have here no lasting home; every earthly family can only image, poorly or well, but always imperfectly, the communion of saints and the divine love eternally generated within the Holy Trinity. This is the love we are made for. Our broken family life blurred the facsimile. But no human love or relationship can satisfy our need for God. *You have made us for Yourself O Lord*, said the great Saint Augustine, *and our hearts are restless until they rest in You*.

I thrilled to hold Olivia for her Baptism; rejoiced at her First Communion; beamed at her Confirmation by Bishop William Curlin, friend to Mother Teresa, who would become, in the last year of his life, a dear friend to me as well.

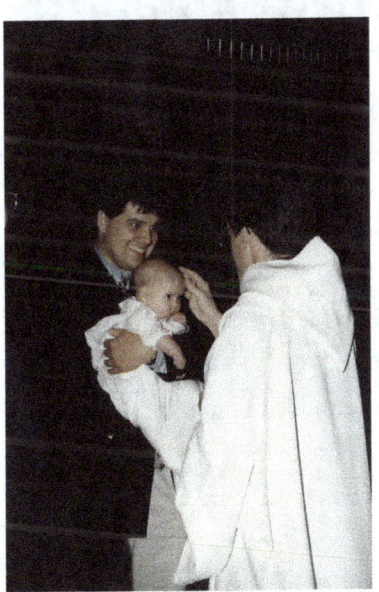

Olivia's baptism, St. Catherine of Siena parish, Manchester, NH

Olivia and Rick at Paradiso, October 2021

I rejoiced that Olivia and Tim had a Catholic education, first at St. Matthew Elementary School, then Holy Trinity Catholic Middle School, and finally Charlotte Catholic High School. We attended Mass together. At home we said grace before meals. Crucifixes, Marian artwork, and the Divine Mercy image adorned the walls.

Olivia rarely confided in me. But in middle school she told me, "I feel very close to the Lord." My heart swelled with joy.

About four years later it sank when Olivia confided in me again. We were enjoying a week of vacation in the seaside community of Chatham on Cape Cod, a few weeks after her high school graduation and before she headed to

Greenville, North Carolina to begin her freshman year at East Carolina University. We were walking the pleasant wooded neighborhood of the home we had rented, abutting a peaceful marsh.

This time Olivia told me she no longer believed in God.

As an adult Olivia would sit quietly for grace and sometimes join us for Mass. But she would not receive Holy Communion, or cross herself, or engage in prayer.

Her lack of faith was not oppositional or argumentative or defiant. It was sad and wistful. It seemed to stem from an inability to reconcile the woundedness of our world with a good God.

A few days before Olivia died, while we were sipping our morning coffee, Melanie shared with me a dream she'd had the night before.

She was riding in the front seat of a car and my parents were in the back. A younger man and an older man had told Melanie how proud they were of me, and Melanie was sharing their compliments with my parents. Melanie understood the men to be associated with Catholic publishing but had no idea who they were.

"Where was I?" I asked.

"I don't know," said Melanie.

"Maybe it was my funeral," I said.

I meant it jokingly, but Melanie looked horrified. "Don't say that!" The dream, which had at first seemed happy and exciting, now took on a somber cast. We stopped talking about it and returned to our coffee.

3

HOTEL

At approximately 10:00 a.m. on May 5, 2022, Melanie and I pulled into the hotel parking lot, passing Olivia's car. We had sped to get here. Now that we had arrived, we paused before heading in. We needed to collect ourselves, to brace for our *Via Dolorosa*.

The hotel had given us a suite across the hall from Olivia where we could gather and wait. We hugged the others and wept and consoled each other as best we could.

My state that morning was one more of shock than crushing grief. A stubbed toe, a toothache, or a paper cut brings pain. Yet the gravest injuries often do not pain, but numb. Pain is a warning sign; when we suffer a terrible, irreparable wound, when the worst conceivable danger has already struck, warnings are useless. Pain, for the moment, subsides. We are left simply dazed and stunned, slowly absorbing the enormity of our loss.

We waited in our hotel room while across the hall, the police conducted their investigation in Olivia's sealed-off room. We were given no access. I wanted desperately to hold Olivia, to fold her into my chest and keep her safe. Yet I also dreaded seeing her, lifeless, frozen *in extremis*. I didn't know if I could stand it. I wasn't given the opportunity to find out.

I wasn't present — she had kept us all away — from her most critical hour.

The first priest to arrive was Father Timothy Reid, pastor of beautiful St. Ann's church. After graduating from college, Olivia had spent a year as a teaching assistant at his parish school. Our whole family knew Father Reid. Seeing him now in his Roman collar was a balm to our wounds. His presence was a silent, visual assurance that the Lord had not abandoned us.

The police, polite but firm, would not let even Father Reid into Olivia's room to anoint her. Father prayed solemnly for Olivia through the door.

Father Reid joined us in our hotel room. The room was fuller now, with our friends Gail Buckley-Barringer and Terry DeMao with us, as well as other family and friends. Sandwiches were spread out on the island of the little kitchen area, some sent up by the hotel, others brought by Gail and Terry. It was another kindness, another gift of love we would see so often during our bereavement.

Before he left Father Reid led us in a Rosary for Olivia. The rhythmic *Hail Marys*, repeated 53 times, soothed us. In our prayer we recommended Olivia to our Blessed Mother, sought the Blessed Mother's intercession, and expressed confidence she had been present in the crucial moments when we were not.

> *Holy Mary, Mother of God*
> *Pray for us sinners*
> *Now and at the hour of our death*

During the Rosary a second priest arrived, Father John Allen. Father Allen was pastor of St. Matthew Catholic Church. For Melanie and I, St. Matthew was a second home. Though we were now members of Divine Saviour, our vibrant country parish across the border in York, South Carolina, we had both been members of St. Matthew in the past, Melanie even serving on the pastoral council. We continued to visit St. Matthew often, for Mass and other events. One of our favorite memories was kneeling side by side at a St. Matthew Holy Hour in 2019, rapt in prayer as we adored Jesus in the Monstrance and listened as the talented parish musicians praised Him in song. It was shortly after this Holy Hour that Melanie and I began dating.

Father Allen hugged Melanie and me and offered his condolences to all. He was pastor of one of the country's largest parishes and had come here directly from a funeral Mass, coincidentally for one of Melanie's childhood friends, Myra Casnettie. He had mind-boggling demands on his time. Yet, like Father Reid, he was fully present, aware of our pastoral needs, and accompanying us through our trial. He did not seem hurried or rushed.

Father Allen walked to Olivia's room, still sealed by police. As Father Reid had done he prayed through the door, this time adding the Apostolic Blessing:

> *By the authority which the Apostolic See has given me, I grant you a full pardon and the remission of all your sins in the name of the Father, and of the Son, and of the Holy Spirit.*

These powerful words were enormously consoling, though there is a mystery to them. Sacraments are for the well-disposed and living. Olivia was, apparently, dead. How could she benefit?

The Church defines death as the definitive separation of the soul from the body. Just when that separation occurs, however, is not easy to determine. It might happen at the last breath, or swiftly thereafter. Or it might happen more slowly, with the soul retaining a connection to the body until corruption sets in.

This opaqueness surrounding the moment of death gives the Church space to act. Priests may administer Last Rites to the apparently deceased conditionally for a short window of time. Especially when death has been sudden, the window is lengthened.

The abruptness of Olivia's death and the questions surrounding it were a cause of anguish for us. At the same time, they were a mercy. The uncertainty about the moment of her passing is precisely what allowed Olivia to receive the Apostolic Blessing — with the hope that her last act in this world was not ingesting the poison that killed her but repenting that act and all else that required repentance and accepting the loving embrace of the Lord.

After Father Allen said the prayers for Olivia he returned to our hotel suite. Our counter of sandwiches was still mostly untouched. Father politely declined our offer to prepare him a plate but encouraged us to keep our normal routines in the face of our shock. "Stay hydrated," he said. "Food's not as important," he added, as I reflexively glanced down at my own ample waistline. "During these next few days, though, make sure you are drinking plenty of water."

Father Allen again assured us of his prayers and said his goodbyes. I walked him to the elevator. Before he pushed the button, he shared that loss of a loved one to suicide was a cross that touched an increasing number of families today — and that the Church was close to them in its pastoral care.

"The *Catechism* gives us great reason to hope in these cases," he said. "So often suicide is an act of depression and mental illness, done without full knowledge and deliberate consent."

The elevator arrived, and Father Allen stepped in. "God bless you, Rick," he said. Then the doors closed. I headed back to the hotel room to wait with Melanie for the police to finish their examination and take Olivia away.

4

CHASMS

There is nothing beautiful about suicide. This needs to be said plainly.

Certain cultures and communities have occasionally seen in suicide something noble and romantic. When the German novelist Johann Goethe published *The Sorrows of Young Werther* in 1774, his literary sensation sparked multiple deaths across Europe. Young, lovelorn men copied the titular character. They pressed guns to their heads and pulled the triggers, believing themselves doomed to perpetual frustration and their self-inflicted deaths heroic.

Death is ugly. My friend Bishop Curlin once ministered to a man teetering on the edge of a building. "I'm going to jump!" the man yelled. Bishop Curlin knew just how to respond. He looked down at the ground and shuddered. "Don't do that. Think of the mess!" He shuddered again. "Who will clean it up?"

The gambit worked. The man looked down, paled at the image the Bishop had given him, and returned inside.

The body, says the Bible, *is sown in dishonour* (1 Cor 15:43). That's a polite way of saying our lifeless bodies, when we bury them, are gruesome. God's original plan for creation had no place for human corpses.

Death can achieve a moral beauty through the acts of the one dying. *Precious in the eyes of the Lord is the death of his saints* (Ps 116:15). Death accepted with trust in the Lord's promise to raise us up, and a desire to intercede in His presence for loved ones left behind, is beautiful. It is a participation in the prayer of Jesus, *Father, into your hands I commend my spirit* (Lk 23:46). It is a laying down of one's life for one's friends.

Suicide in itself is the antithesis of such an act. It does not look with trust to the Lord. It takes the precious gift of one's life and snuffs it — not for the love of neighbor, not as a sacrifice for a greater good, but in the expectation of annihilation, in the hope, literally, of nothing. Suicide, says the *Catechism of the Catholic Church*, "offends love of neighbor" and "breaks ties of solidarity with family." It is "contrary to love for the living God" (CCC 2281).

How then, could I have hope for Olivia, as Father Allen had urged?

How can a suicide be saved?

The *Catechism* offers two grounds for hope. First, as Father Allen had stated, the suicide's moral responsibility can be diminished for several reasons, including depression and mental illness.

Second, a suicide's choice to end life may not be his

or her final choice. "We should not despair of the eternal salvation of persons who have taken their own lives," says the *Catechism*. "By ways known to him alone, God can provide the opportunity for salutary repentance. The Church prays for people who have taken their own lives" (CCC 2283).

An oft-told story from the life of Saint John Vianney illustrates this well. The widow of a man who had committed suicide by jumping off a bridge came to the saint, tormented by the fear her husband was in hell.

Keep praying for your husband, the saint counseled. *Your husband is in purgatory. Between the bridge and the water he repented, and he was saved.*

Olivia suffered from anxiety and depression. I had seen signs of it but did not know its depths. Her suicide note, which the police retrieved from her hotel room and shared with us, offered a glimpse of her inner anguish.

Though I was not included in the note, I did read it. True to her sweet and loving nature, she was more concerned with everyone else than herself.

The mixture of love and empathy for others with self-loathing and a desire for death is jarring and hard to understand. But it not uncommon; I had seen it before. Those suffering from depression and even suicidal ideation are often exceptionally loving people.

I learned this first as a 15-year-old boy when my mother gave me a copy of *The Once and Future King*. I devoured it, especially the book on Lancelot, *The Ill-Made Knight*. Lancelot is the strongest knight and the meekest, kind and considerate to everyone. But his kindness and sensitivity is the fruit of a deep inner pain.

At the conclusion of his book, Lancelot's depression and self-hatred even tempt him to suicide. At the last moment he changes his mind — and works a miracle that showed how he was especially loved by God.

When I was a sophomore at Georgetown, a few years after encountering *The Once and Future King*, I discovered Gerard Manley Hopkins, the great Jesuit priest and poet. I marveled at his innovative use of language and mystical insights and committed several of his poems to heart. Many years later, I would weave some of my favorite Hopkins lines into *Messiah*.

Gerard Manley Hopkins

Hopkins' poetry expresses praise and worship of God with a power and beauty approaching that of the Psalms; some of Hopkins' poetry is even included in the Breviary, the prayer book used daily by priests, deacons, and religious to recite the Divine Office or Liturgy of the Hours.

In addition to his poetry of praise, Hopkins also authored several poems describing his intense internal suffering. These "terrible sonnets" or "sonnets of desolation" express the poet's loss of the sense of God, causing a pain so intense he yearns for the cessation of consciousness, as in this passage from the sonnet *No Worst, There Is None*.

O the mind, mind has mountains; cliffs of fall
Frightful, sheer, no-man-fathomed. Hold them cheap,
May, who ne'er hung there. Nor does long our small
Durance deal with that steep or deep. Here! creep,
Wretch, under a comfort serves in a whirlwind: all
Life death does end and each day dies with sleep.

In another poem, *Carrion Comfort*, Hopkins again chronicles the struggle against despair, the desire not-to-be:

Not, I'll not, carrion comfort, Despair, not feast on thee;
Not untwist — slack they may be — these last strands of man
In me ór, most weary, cry I can no more. I can;
Can something, hope, wish day come, not choose not to be.

Hopkins resisted the temptation to cry *I can no more*. He persevered through years of depression and feeling alienated from God, dying of typhoid fever at age 44. In his final moments of life, his depression lifted, and the day he wished for seemed to have come. His last words were "I am happy, so happy. I loved my life."

For some mysterious reason, the Providence of God allowed Olivia to share with Hopkins an inner landscape of frightful chasms from which she hung. Unlike Hopkins, she did not persevere in clinging; after years of depression she let go.

My prayer was that between letting go and the bottom, between the chasm and the pit, Olivia grasped the outstretched arms of the Lord, that He got her, and that she died *happy, so happy* too.

But there was an opacity to these moments, to the hour of her death, as sealed from my scrutiny as was her lifeless body in the hotel room where she died.

How could I know what happened to Olivia? On what grounds could I hope?

5

MERCY

Saint Faustina Kowalska was a Polish nun born in 1915. During her short life, she experienced frequent visions and communications from Jesus. At the prompting of her spiritual director, Faustina recorded her encounters with the Lord and other mystical experiences in a diary. Published after her death at age 33 in 1938, *Divine Mercy in My Soul* became a worldwide bestseller. Over one million copies of Faustina's diary have been distributed in multiple languages to date.

Saint Faustina's experiences and *Diary* are the source of the Divine Mercy devotion — an invitation from Jesus to contemplate His profound Mercy, poured out for all from the Cross, and to invoke it for oneself and others.

The devotion is comprised of various elements. These include the Feast of Mercy, specific prayers, and the Divine Mercy image. This well-known picture portrays the Risen Christ with rays of light streaming from His heart, representing the blood and water which flowed from His pierced side on the Cross. Written at the bottom of the image is the phrase *Jesus, I Trust in You*.

I knew nothing of the Divine Mercy devotion until I encountered it through my work in Catholic publishing at age 25. As for the mystery of God's Mercy, I had grappled with it from an early age.

One of my dearest friends as a young boy was my cousin Chris. Just nine months my junior, we shared a school grade, an enthusiasm for comic books and penny candy, and a love of outdoor adventures. Chris lived about a 40-minute drive from my family's home in Stoneham. We saw each other every few months: for Sunday dinners at our grandparent's house in Jamaica Plain; gatherings at the Cape Cod home owned by our generous great-uncle and great-aunt; and during summer days by the lake in Wolfeboro, New Hampshire, hometown of our great-grandfather and, for his descendants, another beloved vacation spot.

Mine was a happy childhood. I was blessed with a large, loving extended family on both my mother's and father's side. When Chris was present at a family event my happiness swelled to near-unbridled excitement and joy. Often we'd conspire to extend our time together, pleading that one of us be allowed to go back with the other for a few days of extended fun.

It was during one of these times when I was six or seven years old that Chris told me his father, my Uncle John, was leaving the home he shared with my Aunt Sarah, Chris, and my cousins Mary and Lisa.

"I forget the word for it," Chris told me matter-of-factly.

"You mean, divorce?" I said, my heart sinking. "Yes," said Chris, "that's it."

John's abandonment of Sarah and their family was the greatest tragedy I knew — the first sight of the serpent in my childhood Eden. Later the serpent would show his fangs even more. By the time I was ten, I learned that John had left to lead an actively homosexual life. He was one of the early casualties of AIDS, dying after much suffering in 1987 when I was 18.

As a boy I prayed every night for John. I wrestled with God for him like Jacob. To this day I have never prayed more strongly. I pleaded with God to send John back to Sarah, Mary, Chris and Lisa. I implored Him to restore their family. And I begged God to forgive John's offenses, to remember his service as an altar boy, his good intentions in marriage, and the extenuating circumstances and life events that may have derailed him from his desired course.

I continued my intense prayer regimen for months. It had no apparent effect. John did not go back to his family. Until AIDS sapped his strength he didn't change his life.

When John died in 1987, however, it was in the arms of the Church, with a large Catholic funeral after receiving the Last Rites.

When I was about 12 years old, I had what I believe was another encounter with God's mercy. It began with a dream. I was taken by a special Willie Wonka-type elevator to a place that was otherwise inaccessible to me. There I met a nun dressed in black. *You better pray for your Papa*, she told me.

I'm not in the habit of sharing my dreams, or even remembering them. This one I did. I began a new prayer intention and told my parents about the dream so I could enlist their prayers too. I called my beloved paternal grandfather *Papa*, so I prayed for him. But I wondered if the mysterious nun might have meant by *Papa* my own Dad, or my maternal grandfather, Grandpa. To be safe I prayed for them all.

Three years later Papa died suddenly and unexpectedly of a heart attack at age 75. He was a wonderful man, a pillar of the community, a faithful churchgoer, devoted to my Nana, his sons, grandchildren and entire family. He too had a large Catholic funeral, with hundreds attending.

Yet in every life there is a need for mercy, for healing. Papa had died with the wounds from a painful rift with his sisters still festering. And his sudden death prevented his receiving the Last Rites.

It was a grace and comfort to have prayed for him before he died, at the prompting of my dream-encounter with the nun dressed in black.

Who was she? And does such a question even make sense?

The nun was a character from a dream. She appeared with other images obviously derived from my own reading and memory and experience, such as the Willie Wonka-like elevator that brought me to her. The obvious answer is she was a projection of my subconscious.

Still, I was intrigued. As a 12-year-old boy attending public school in Stoneham, Massachusetts in 1980, I didn't know many nuns, and none who wore black. If she were manufactured by my own imagination, I hadn't provided much in the way of raw material. Then too the nun had seemed to warn me, in a subtle way, of the impending but unforeseen death of Papa. She had prepared me for the most traumatic death of my young life — a death that would retain that grim ranking for 38 years.

A few years after Papa's death I told Nana about the dream. "Did Papa have any special nuns in his life?" I asked her. He had. As a boy, he'd had religious sisters as teachers. One took a special interest in him. When they met again when Papa was an adult, Sister asked if he was still going to Mass. He wasn't, but her question pricked Papa's conscience, and he began attending Mass again. Thereafter, he did so faithfully every Sunday with Nana until he died.

Saint Faustina Kowalska

Ten years after Papa's death I was early in my career in Catholic publishing. Our Northern Virginia operation included a wonderful Catholic bookstore. There I discovered spiritual treasures I would cherish for life: the music of John Michael Talbot; Eucharistic Exposition and Benediction; and the diary of a nun dressed in black, Saint Faustina's *Divine Mercy in My Soul*.

Over my next 25 years in Catholic publishing I would change publishing houses and projects. My work included Bibles and prayer books, children's books and video education courses, coffee table books, literary criticism, and papal biographies. But there was always a pull to the Divine Mercy.

In the early 2000s I was working for the Bible publisher Stampley. Our "World's Most Beautiful" Family Bibles were famous for their devotional sections on the Life of Christ, the Rosary, and the Stations of the Cross. Why not add one on the Divine Mercy too? I reached out to the Marians, official promoters of the Divine Mercy. They thought it a great idea and designed the 16-page insert for us. Later they gave their blessing as we created the original "Divine Mercy Bible," with a stunning print of the Divine Mercy image affixed to the cover.

In April 2015 I was working for the publisher Saint Benedict Press, parent company of TAN Books. When Pope Francis proclaimed the following year would be a "Jubilee of Mercy" — the first of its kind in the history of the Church — I was filled with excitement. We immediately rolled up our sleeves and got to work, producing an 8-part video series, *Doors of Mercy*, to help others observe the Jubilee year and learn about the Divine Mercy devotion. In 2016 *Doors of Mercy* was studied in hundreds of parishes. On March 16, 2016, I was able to hand deliver a copy to Pope Francis at a General Audience in Rome and speak a few words.

"Thank you for the Jubilee Year, Holy Father," I said as I grasped his hand and kissed the Fisherman's ring.

"Pray for me," he replied, as he looked at me and smiled. Then he added, with a twinkle in his eye, "Don't forget!"

Rick (lower right) at General Audience with Pope Francis, March 16, 2016

That encounter with the Holy Father planted the seeds of a future project, *Messiah*. In 2018 I led a group of 17 professionals and pilgrims to the Holy Land and Rome to film *Messiah* at almost 30 different locations. The filming expedition was the adventure of a lifetime and a source of enormous blessings.

The biggest blessing was the friendship I developed with one of the pilgrims, Melanie. Melanie shared my passion for *Messiah* and volunteered to assist with production, filming and distribution. By the end of 2019 my work on *Messiah* was largely over — but my desire to spend time with Melanie was not. We began dating and married on May 26, 2021, the Feast of Saint Philip Neri.

Patti Defilippis, Melanie, and Father John O'Brien, S.J., filming in Jerusalem for Messiah

Messiah tells the story of Jesus, showing how He is foretold by "Moses and all the prophets," and how Scripture is fulfilled in His life, ministry, Passion, and in the establishment and growth of the Church. Though *Messiah* focuses on the messianic prophecies of the Bible, the story of Jesus is necessarily the story of Divine Mercy and the ineffable power of the Cross. I incorporated elements of the Divine Mercy devotion into *Messiah* in subtle ways.

My love of the Divine Mercy devotion and promotion of its

message over the years did not, alas, mean I regularly prayed the Chaplet. I venerated the Divine Mercy image; I loved and observed the Feast of Mercy, celebrated on the first Sunday after Easter, but I rarely prayed the Divine Mercy prayers that Jesus gave to Saint Faustina, prayed on regular rosary beads and requiring just a few minutes each day.

Why? I can only confess I am an unprofitable servant. The ardent prayer regimen I had offered for John as a boy over many months had been exhausting, and I was afraid of experiencing such exhaustion again.

I drew much from Saint Therese of Lisieux's words in her spiritual memoir, *Story of a Soul:*

> "I have not the courage to look through books for beautiful prayers. I only get a headache because of their number...Unable therefore to say them all, and lost in choice, I do as children who have not learnt to read — I simply tell Our Lord all that I want, and He always understands."[2]

I made less of the fact that these words were written by one who longed to pour herself out for souls, to take on all the torments of the martyrs for the love of Jesus[3]. Love sacrifices for the beloved, and persistence in a prayer regimen is a very mild form of that sacrifice and an expression of love. But I did not undertake it. I am an unprofitable servant.

In the weeks before Olivia died, however, by the grace of God, I would be invited to pray the Divine Mercy Chaplet in an extraordinary way.

Melanie and I had planned to lead a pilgrimage to the Holy Land for Pentecost, with our dear friend Father Mark Lawlor of St. Therese Catholic Church in Mooresville. Israel had only recently reopened after the Covid lockdowns, and we'd had a very short window to recruit pilgrims. Our April 11 deadline for signing pilgrims was just nine days away. We were still far off from our minimum and very discouraged.

On April 2, at 2 p.m., I made the acquaintance by phone of Tom, a parishioner at St. Therese. Tom had a leg ailment that made it difficult to walk all but the shortest distances and left him in chronic pain. Candidly, he was not a good candidate for a pilgrimage. But he passionately desired to go and had an idea to help us meet our minimum.

"Have you considered praying the Divine Mercy Chaplet for the intention of the Holy Land pilgrimage?" he asked. "How about we do it as a group and invite others to join us in saying it at 3 o'clock?"

Three o'clock, the "Hour of Mercy," has a special significance in the Divine Mercy devotion. It is the hour when Jesus died (cf Mt 27:46).

"Jesus told Saint Faustina whatever we ask of Him at the Hour of Mercy He cannot refuse."

Tom's declaration — *whatever we ask of Jesus at the Hour of Mercy He cannot refuse* — seemed imbued with an unexpected authority. In my state of discouragement, these words were a lifeline. I seized them. "All right, Tom, great idea! We'll pray the Divine Mercy Chaplet every day at 3 p.m. for the next nine days, for the intention of a successful Holy Land pilgrimage, starting today." I got off the phone with Tom, then called my magnanimous parents to enlist them once again in our prayer campaign. Melanie and I called our friends Gail and Steve as well, who generously offered to join our nine day prayer regimen, too. At 3 p.m. we prayed our first Chaplet.

Over the next nine days we continued. We were heartened by new pilgrim registrations and inquiries. We completed our nine days of prayer on April 11 — Monday of Holy Week, and our deadline.

Even with the new registrations, we hadn't met our minimum. Our travel partner, Canterbury Pilgrimages, graciously granted us an extension. We continued praying our 3 p.m. Chaplets. For Melanie, extending novenas was second nature; as a girl her mother had taught her to always follow nine days of petition with nine days of thanksgiving, a "novena of gratitude," as an act of faith in God's Providence. In this spirit we continued, hopeful that within nine additional days we'd register the additional pilgrims we needed.

On April 15, Good Friday, we added to our daily Chaplets the Novena intentions given to Saint Faustina by Jesus. We began a Divine Mercy Novena in its fullest sense, scheduled to end on Divine Mercy Sunday. Now we were praying in solidarity with faithful around the world, adding to our personal intention those of the Lord and His Church.

We observed the Easter Triduum and continued our prayers. Easter is the most important Feast in the Church — and the one with the most Mass attendance. We hoped some of the additional worshippers in local parishes would register and bring us to our minimum. It was not to be. On April 20, Wednesday of Easter Week, Melanie and I made the difficult decision to postpone our pilgrimage. Jesus had not answered our petition for a successful Holy Land pilgrimage in the manner we had hoped.

Nevertheless, we continued our Divine Mercy Novena to its conclusion on Divine Mercy Sunday, April 24. That day Melanie and I attended the 12:30 p.m. Mass at St. Matthew. We were fortunate to be among the last two penitents to receive Confession, minutes before Mass began.

That meant we fulfilled, at the last moment, one of the conditions of the Divine Mercy promise given to Saint Faustina by Jesus: Whoever receives Communion on Divine Mercy Sunday, having been recently confessed, shall receive total remission of all sins and punishments.

The Divine Mercy Mass was beautiful, enriched by the participation of the seminarians from Charlotte's St. Joseph Seminary, and the unexpected presence of my son, Tim, with whom we were delighted to share our pew. We relished St. Matthew's beautiful music, listened attentively to the prayers and readings, and rose as the Gospel was proclaimed.

Every year, the Gospel reading for Divine Mercy Sunday is the same, taken from chapter 20 of the Gospel according to Saint John.

It tells of Jesus' first encounter with the apostles after His Resurrection. All of them except John have abandoned Jesus. They are fearful and ashamed.

Jesus comes to them anyway, unhindered by the locked doors of the Upper Room, or Cenacle, where they are hiding. *Peace be with you*, He says.

When Thomas is told of the appearance he refuses to believe

it, not wanting his hopes dashed again. Jesus comes to him too. *Put your finger here...and do not be unbelieving, but believe.*

What a beautiful example of the Mercy of God! As He did for the apostles, Jesus comes to us, even when we have locked the doors of our heart, even when we have closed ourselves through fear or disappointment or shame. He seeks out the lost sheep. He stands before us and knocks. He invites us into His vineyard, not once but multiple times, up until the very close of day.

As Melanie and I received Holy Communion that Sunday, we thanked God for His promise of the complete remission of sins which He had made through Saint Faustina. We silently offered the grace we had received to Our Lady, to apply to any soul as she deemed best.

After Mass, Melanie and I had dinner with Tim at Firebirds. We went home happy, despite our disappointment that our Novena for a successful Holy Land pilgrimage had seemingly failed.

We had no idea then that in just 10 days, Olivia would embark on her own perilous pilgrimage and would need Divine Mercy to bring her home.

6

I'VE GOT HER!

On May 6, the day after we found Olivia, I awoke from sleep to confront Olivia's death anew. It was a recurring experience in the weeks and months to follow, a fleeting moment of refreshment and feeling that *all's right with the world*, incinerated by the red-hot poker jab of memory,[4] the forced acknowledgment that Olivia was no longer in it.

William Wordsworth describes this experience in his sonnet *Surprised by Joy.* The poem is perhaps best known today for providing the title to C.S. Lewis' spiritual memoir of the same name. Those familiar with the connection might expect Wordsworth's sonnet to explore how God draws us to Himself through beauty. The poem, however, is actually a lament for Wordsworth's daughter, Lucy. It describes his pain not only at her death but also at *recalling* her death after a moment's reprieve:

Surprised by joy — impatient as the Wind
I turned to share the transport — Oh! with whom
But Thee, long buried in the silent Tomb,
That spot which no vicissitude can find?
Love, faithful love, recalled thee to my mind —
But how could I forget thee? Through what power,
Even for the least division of an hour,
Have I been so beguiled as to be blind
To my most grievous loss! That thought's return
Was the worst pang that sorrow ever bore,
Save one, one only, when I stood forlorn,
Knowing my heart's best treasure was no more;
That neither present time, nor years unborn
Could to my sight that heavenly face restore.

I would come to know well the pang of continually confronting Olivia's death, shouldering its weight as it dug into fresh areas of my life. The magnitude of loss was so great I could assimilate it only over months, through repeated inner assents over time.

I did not bear my burden alone. Every step of my *Via Crucis* Melanie was beside me, holding me, supporting me, bringing comfort. Her love was strong and passionate, practical and anticipatory. She made sure, as Father Allen had warned, that I did not neglect to eat or drink — and even occasionally made the drink a glass of wine to make a grieving heart glad. She cheerfully handled all household affairs, and managed funeral and hosting and travel arrangements when I was too stunned to engage.

LOVE IS STRONGER THAN DEATH

Melanie and I had been married less than a year.

Rick and Melanie's Wedding Reception at Paradiso, May 26, 2021

Our Nuptial Mass at little Divine Saviour parish was concelebrated by four priest-friends of the Rock Hill Oratory, which had built and staffed the parishes of York County and surrounding communities since 1934. In honor of our beloved Oratorians, we'd chosen the Feast Day of their Founder, Saint Philip Neri, as our wedding date. A television miniseries about Saint Philip, *Preferisco il Paradiso* ("I Prefer Heaven") provided the name for our home.

Saint Philip Neri is known as the "Saint of Joy" and the "Second Apostle of Rome." Like Saint Philip Neri, Melanie and I wanted to be apostles, too, fostering joy, beauty, and fellowship through our marriage and work with Cenacle. Olivia's suicide entered our happy vision with the force of the *strepitus* at a Tenebrae service. Melanie did not flee this cross but carried it with me, never doubting that all things work together for the good of those who love Him (Rom 8:28).

I also had consolation from many friends. One of them was Bob Gallagher, Conor's father, a Catholic publisher and businessman who played a role in many Catholic initiatives here, including salvaging TAN Books from bankruptcy, launching, with his partner James Hetzel, The Catholic Company, and revitalizing the Order of Malta in the Charlotte region. Bob has earned many accolades in his life but the most apt is the one Conor conferred on him at his 50th birthday celebration: *Man of the Church.*

Bob and James had brought me and my family to Charlotte in 1999. Bob and I had worked on many Catholic projects together, and though he was no longer my employer, he sent me the following email just hours after we learned of Olivia's death.

> I am so very sorry to hear about Olivia. Please

know that I offered Mass today for her and for
you. Our faith teaches us that now she is at
peace. I know she had her struggles but I also
know two other things. She was a good young
lady and you were an excellent father. Only God
knows the depths of her pain and her internal
battles. But, you can rest assured that He saw
through her depression to the beautiful young
lady she is. I use the word is because she still
is. She is now living on a different and better
plane with the very Savior you introduced her to.
Please try to take some comfort in the knowledge
that she is at peace. Tomorrow morning Abbot
Placid is offering our Malta First Friday mass for
Olivia, for you and your family. You remain in my
prayers and in the prayers of your confreres. If I
can help in any way please let me know.

Another consoler was Conor. Conor had called me when Olivia was still missing, minutes after the email distribution requesting prayers. That same evening, he'd come to the house to share, grieve and reminisce.

Conor had known Olivia since she was not yet three, and he was a 20-year-old student at Steubenville. Weeks after I moved to Charlotte, and having never met, we bumped into each other at the community park at my Ballantyne apartment, where I played with Olivia and Conor chatted with a friend.

Olivia's happy but nonsensical prattling — *Dikka Dikka Doo! Dikka Dikka Doo!* — caught Conor's attention. He remarked on it with delight. I introduced myself and we soon realized our connection. Olivia had brought us together; now she was bringing us together again.

At Paradiso, Conor joined me and Melanie and a small group of friends who had also come to be with us. We shared a meal, and when we first paused to say grace, Conor asked to lead it. He added a few words about me.

"You were a great father, Rick. Never forget that."

Conor is experienced in fatherhood as are few others; he and his beautiful wife Ashley are the parents of 16 children. He had witnessed my own fathering up close, and knew of the strains and fault lines in my relationship with Olivia. His words, and Bob's, were a balm offered to prevent needless regret and anxiety infecting the wound of my grief.

After dinner Conor and I chatted and looked out over the beautiful pasture and woodland from Paradiso's back patio. We talked about some of TAN's publishing activities, including TAN's book of the year, *Trustful Surrender to Divine Providence*, a spiritual classic by Saint Claude de la Colombière that reflects on how everything that happens in our lives, without exception, is ordained or allowed by the mercy of God for our good.

"Pay attention to the way God is working in your life through Olivia's death," Conor advised me. "Be alert for signs of His presence."

Conor's words stayed with me the next morning as Melanie and I prepared our breakfast and drank our coffee on our front porch. After breakfast, Melanie and I set out on the hour-long drive to Weddington to Heritage Funeral Home to make arrangements for Olivia.

View from back deck over Paradiso

We had been with Olivia just days ago. It was less than 24 hours since we'd learned she'd died. We hadn't seen her ill, had not yet seen her deceased. Now we were planning her funeral. It felt surreal.

Melanie and I pulled into the parking lot at Heritage. We were welcomed by the Funeral Director, Karen.

"Good morning!" Karen beckoned us to follow as she moved from the reception area through a showroom of caskets and coffins to the door of a Conference Room. "We'll be meeting here to discuss the arrangements for Olivia."

We seated ourselves and were soon joined by Mary Catherine Surface, another pillar of the Church in Charlotte, rich in good works and a family friend. Mary Catherine generously accompanied us during this difficult time and helped us navigate Olivia's funeral planning.

As I looked around the table at Mary Catherine, the family and close friends, I felt the consolation of these faithful women and marveled at the mercy of God, who never lets us be tried beyond our strength to endure (1 Cor 10:13).

We spent the morning making Olivia's arrangements. There was a lot to arrange: a coffin and casket for Olivia; decorative casket plaques; floral presentations; a memorial prayer card and Bible verse. We also had to settle on times for Olivia's wake, to be held the night before the funeral at Heritage, and for the funeral, which we hoped to hold in St. Matthew's main sanctuary.

By 11:30 a.m. we had made most of our decisions. We prepared to break for lunch, and then head to St. Matthew to go over the funeral details with St. Matthew staff.

Before we left, while we were sitting around the conference table, Mary Catherine shared a story.

"Rick, I almost forgot to tell you and Melanie something that happened yesterday!" Mary Catherine's face was glowing.

"I heard from a friend named Diane, a parishioner at St. Ann. When we sent out the email requesting prayers for Olivia yesterday morning, I also texted Diane at the same time."

"I don't usually include Diane on this kind of distribution list," Mary Catherine continued, "but for some reason I was prompted to include her at the last moment. Diane received my text requesting prayers right before heading into Daily Mass at St. Ann, knowing only that Olivia was missing. She prayed for Olivia at Mass and offered her Holy Communion for her. At that moment, Diane felt the Lord reassure her and speak to her soul."

"I've got her, Diane. I've got her."

Mary Catherine's story cut me to the core.

I've got her.

It was the same assurance I had received yesterday before we found Olivia. It was the same phrase I had shared with Melanie as we sped to the hotel.

I had interpreted these words then as a promise we would find Olivia alive. When we learned Olivia was dead I dismissed them as wishful thinking, a defense mechanism against grief.

But in Diane's experience at Holy Communion, I found confirmation of my own — and a far more profound meaning to the words *I've got her* than I originally allowed.

Melanie and I said our goodbyes at the funeral home, grabbed a quick lunch, then reconvened with the others at St. Matthew.

The priests and staff at St. Matthew accompanied us every step of the way as we planned Olivia's funeral. It would be held in five days, on Wednesday, May 11, giving time for distant family to arrive. St. Matthew allowed us an afternoon rather than the normal late morning funeral, so that, in a nod to the Divine Mercy devotion, we could bury Olivia during the "Hour of Mercy" beginning at 3 p.m. Above all St. Matthew gave us the parish's main sanctuary, rather than the smaller Daily Mass Chapel. Olivia's would be the first funeral held there since the start of the pandemic.

The Lord is near to the brokenhearted and saves the crushed in spirit (Ps 34:8). We experienced that in full at St. Matthew. Melanie said it more colorfully. "St. Matthew rolled out the red carpet for us."

After a full day of planning, Melanie and I left St. Matthew for the hour-long drive home.

Shortly after we arrived, around 6 p.m., we saw something we had never seen before: A full rainbow arching over Paradiso, spanning and encompassing the entire property.

The rainbow seemed another confirmation of Diane's words, a symbolic rendering of them writ high across the sky.

Rainbow over Paradiso May 6, 2022, the day after Olivia died

7

ANGELS

The word "angel" comes from the Greek word *angelos*, meaning "messenger." In the days surrounding Olivia's death we seemed to receive many extraordinary messages, including Melanie's funeral dream; Tom's urging us to pray a Divine Mercy Novena; the rainbow over Paradiso; and the words Diane heard from the Lord — *I've got her* — which I separately had felt pressed upon my soul.

Were these events in fact messages from another — from Olivia, from an angel, from Saint Faustina, and ultimately from God?

Or were they simply events from ordinary life, into which I read a significance that wasn't there?

The mind is a strange and powerful faculty. I'd seen with Olivia how it can shape experiences and memories to fit a narrative. Olivia had found a way, in the face of her beauty and goodness, to rationalize self-loathing. I did not doubt I was capable of the reverse. I could subconsciously create something beautiful to mask the ugliness of death. In the Sahara of grief I could manufacture a mirage.

The messages we received in connection with Olivia's death, however, did not seem internally generated. Daydreams are soft and pliable. The messages, in contrast, had a resistance and "otherness" about them. They erupted forcefully and unexpectedly. They commanded our attention and seemed imbued with meaning but did not initially reveal their full or true significance.

Saints Monica and Augustine.

In his *Confessions* Saint Augustine describes different imaginative visions experienced by his mother, Saint Monica.

Monica hoped for a Christian marriage for her son. Some of her visions seemed to promise just that. But Monica was never very confident in these visions, feeling somehow that they were, as Augustine writes, "dreams of her own spirit." [5]

A dream she had almost nine years before Augustine's conversion was different. In this dream Monica was standing on a wooden rule, symbolizing the rule of faith. She was sorrowful and downcast. A beautiful young man, perhaps an angel, approached her.

Why are you so sad? he asked. Monica replied she was grieving for her son, who had rejected the faith. She looked more closely at the youth. She thought it was Augustine.

Don't grieve, he told her joyfully, *for where you are, I also shall be.*

Monica held fast to those words for nine years, convinced they were from God. When she first told Augustine about them, he dismissed them. He even said Monica should fear they prophesied Monica would become a Manichean.

Monica wasn't swayed. *I wasn't told that I would join you, but that you would join me*, she said. Augustine was moved. The calm assurance and steadfastness the dream produced in his mother impressed him more than the dream itself.[6]

Saint Monica's hope for Augustine was my one hope now for Olivia. I would never give her away at her wedding, dandle her children, see her enter a profession, embrace a vocation, establish a home. But I could hope that *where she is, I also will be*. I could pray that we would one day be united — more so than we had ever been on earth — praising the Lord in Heaven with all the angels and saints.

In the days after Olivia died the messages of reassurance continued, as friends and loved ones reached out. We received flowers and Facebook condolences, texts and letters, beautiful books and poems to help us grieve, and, from one old friend a silly gift to make us laugh. My thoughtful cousin Beth sent rosemary plants as a living reminder of Olivia. My cousin Jeanne planted a tree in her memory.

These gestures were consoling and often accompanied by promises of prayer. I was enormously grateful. It wasn't just myself praying for Olivia or our family, but Christ in His Mystical Body interceding on her behalf.

This was true above all in the dozens of Masses offered for Olivia. Each one was a holy and living sacrifice offered to the Father, a prayer for Divine Mercy in its perfect form: *For the sake of His sorrowful Passion, have mercy on Olivia and on the whole world.*

Prayer transcends time. Saint Padre Pio once told a friend, speaking of his long-dead great-grandfather, *even now I can pray for his happy death*. God exists in an eternal now, explained the saint, not bound by our linear experience of past, present and future. He takes into account, at the moment of death, prayers that will be, but have not yet been, said.[7]

God knew from all eternity the prayers and Masses that would be offered for Olivia. He took them into account. They were with Olivia in her final moments in the hotel room, a warm beckoning and loving encouragement to accept the Lord's embrace. And they were with us in our grief, a rod and a staff to lean on, a sign of the Spirit coming to aid us in our weakness, taking up our intercessory prayers for Olivia and making them his own (cf. Rom 8:26-27).

One of those praying for Olivia was Father Dennis Kuhn, the chaplain of Holy Angels where Olivia had worked.

Olivia had started at Holy Angels two years earlier. She had applied at my encouragement. I knew it was a special place. Friends from the Order of Malta served on the Board. I had visited Holy Angels, too. I had been present for the Annual Blessing, during which members of the Order spend time with the residents and bring them holy water from Lourdes.

Father Dennis texted me shortly after Olivia started part-time work at Holy Angels in the summer of 2020.

> *Rick: Your daughter Olivia is wonderful. I met her at our New Hire Orientation; I talked with her last night while she was working and she loves her work...Such a beautiful girl. Glad she is sharing in our mission of embracing the values of sacredness of life and human dignity.*

I was grateful for Father Dennis' text when I received it and proud that Olivia's love for the residents was so apparent.

I knew Olivia cared for the residents. She lived with me during much of her time working at Holy Angels, simultaneously studying online for her Master's in Counseling. Our relationship was strained, and though Olivia was always gentle and polite, I had difficulty drawing her into conversation.

One exception was when she had news of her Holy Angels charges. She relished sharing stories about the residents, describing humorous interactions and exchanges with visitors and staff. When the residents suffered from illness or loneliness or anxiety, Olivia suffered too.

I didn't know, however, how central Holy Angels was to Olivia. When she told me at our barbecue on May 1, *sometimes I wish I could just work at Holy Angels,* I was surprised. Olivia repeated the sentiment to Melanie separately that same day. Melanie was surprised too.

"We must know that we have been created for greater things," taught Mother Teresa. "Not just to be a number in the world, not just to go for diplomas and degrees, this work and that work. We have been created in order to love and to be loved."[8]

At Holy Angels, Olivia loved and was loved. That was true, too, of course, with Melanie and me, and with all her family and friends. In these environments, however, there could also be competition, expectations, and automatic self-measuring against peers. At Holy Angels, there was none of that — just loving and being loved.

My eyes were opened to this by Father Dennis when I informed him Olivia had died. Father immediately promised to remember Olivia in his Masses and gave thanks for Olivia's loving care. When I asked him if he could share a brief remembrance of Olivia he responded almost immediately with a glowing tribute. It reads in part:

> Olivia was a precious gift of life and love to the residents of Holy Angels. Her smile, her tender touch, her commitment to quality care, her ability to focus and be present to their needs was so inspiring...She was truly...a living angel

> delivering a message of hope and comfort…Olivia found her calling in service to the Lord. What a wonderful gift of her life before her heavenly home.

To this beautiful remembrance of Olivia Father Dennis appended a personal message to me:

> *Written with tears of sorrow and joy. Like the Holy Rosary, there is twice as much joy in the Mysteries as sorrow. Five for sorrow; ten for joy. Olivia is sharing in the true peace of God that passes all understanding.*

Early Sunday morning, Mother's Day, Melanie went outside to seek solace in nature. Paradiso is blessed with birdlife; this morning their songs and chirps were like nothing she had heard before. A mourning dove called out its note of lament. Joining the dove were a chorus of song birds, praising God.

The pattern was the same one Father Dennis had discerned in the Rosary. *One part sorrow, two parts joy.* Melanie took out her phone to record the moment on video. As she did so, the wind blew softly, stirring our wind chimes to add *sotto voce* the chords of *Amazing Grace.* That day Melanie shared the video on Facebook.

"Just lifting all up to God in prayer," she posted, "and I realize this symphony of the birds is His embrace to my soul."

Mourning dove at Paradiso

8

CHAPEL

On May 11, one-half hour before her funeral, I knelt alone with Olivia in St. Matthew's daily Mass chapel. Our Lord was in the Tabernacle in front of us. The chapel's Divine Mercy image was installed off to the side.

Olivia's wake had been the evening before, at Heritage Funeral Home. It was the first time we had seen Olivia since her last visit to Paradiso.

There she had been happy, vibrant, and laughing. Now she was cold and still. It had wrung my heart to see her, but it was consoling, too. Parents express love for their children in part by seeing that they are well-clothed and groomed. We'd done this for Olivia when she was a little girl; now, in making her burial preparations, we were doing it one last time.

At the wake, before we received our friends, colleagues, and neighbors, our close family had gathered for some time with Olivia alone. At the end of our private time, we had knelt before

Olivia's casket and sang the Divine Mercy Chaplet, our closest friends and family joining in response:

> *For the sake of His sorrowful Passion*
> *Have mercy on us, and on the whole world*

We entrusted Olivia to God's Mercy then. Now I was doing it again, in His Presence.

St. Matthew Chapel

The Lord giveth, says Job in the Bible, *and the Lord taketh away. Blessed be the name of the Lord* (Job 1:21). Job's heart-wrung prayers are sometimes used in funerals, and he is a model for Christians in responding to bereavement and loss. Job felt his afflictions fiercely. Yet they did not overwhelm him or lead him to *grieve like those who have no hope* (1 Thess 4:13).

Job believed his Redeemer lived (Job 19:25) and that death has therefore lost its sting (1 Cor 15:55). If the Lord in His

Providence deprives us of something — or *someone* — precious, it is for the sake of a greater good.

Painful as Olivia's death was, I believed this. In the chapel I silently expressed this trust in prayer.

> *Lord, thank you for taking Olivia to Yourself.*
> *You could have saved her in the hotel room.*
> *You could have stopped her from going.*
> *For some reason You didn't.*
> *I trust this is because You willed a greater good —*
> *for Olivia in her last moments to cling to You*
> *and become a saint.*
> *This is the end we are born for.*
> *Jesus, I trust that through Your Mercy*
> *Olivia achieved it.*
> *I believe You invited me to pray for this*
> *in the Divine Mercy Novena initiated by Tom*
> *And I believe You have assured us*
> *that Olivia is with You*
> *in the "I've got her!" message Diane received*
> *in the rainbow over Paradiso*
> *in Bob Gallagher's email*
> *in Father Dennis' text*
> *in the prayers of your people*
> *in the Masses offered on her behalf*
> *and through the grace of having Olivia's body*
> *in Your presence now.*

I paused and looked at the Divine Mercy image off to my side.

In 1931, Jesus appeared to Saint Faustina, a young, cloistered nun, and instructed her to have His image painted. Four years later the first Divine Mercy painting was publicly unveiled at a shrine in Vilnius, Lithuania. Today, the image is venerated in thousands of churches and millions of homes. The miraculous spread of the Divine Mercy image points to the Lord's thirst for souls, His desire that all trust in Him.

In her *Diary* (1486), Jesus tells Saint Faustina He comes to despairing souls up to three times, with all the graces needed for salvation, with "all the treasures of My Heart." If a soul "shows even a flicker of good will, the mercy of God will accomplish the rest."[9]

Olivia had been a despairing soul. Jesus had come for her too. What was that moment like?

Of course this is something I had and have no power of knowing, at least this side of Heaven. I believed I had an inkling, though, in the experience of Roy Schoeman, a Jewish convert to Catholicism and an author and evangelist who I was blessed to feature in *Messiah*.

As a young man and before his conversion, Roy experienced a mystical encounter with Christ — though Roy did not know Him to be Christ at the time.

Roy is a graduate of both MIT and Harvard Business School. He had achieved exceptional academic and business success. Inside, however, his life was one of spiritual desolation. Though he had been fervent in his youth, he had lost his belief in God. Life seemed pointless.

Roy's one solace came through nature. One day he was walking in a wooded area of Cape Cod, when all the world fell away.

> I felt myself in the immediate presence of God. I was aware of His infinite exaltedness, and of His infinite and personal love for me. I saw my life as though I was looking back on it after death...I saw that every action I had ever done mattered, for good or for evil. I saw that everything which had ever happened in my life had been perfectly designed for my own good from the infinitely wise and loving hand of God, not only including but especially those things which I at the time thought had been the greatest catastrophes.
>
> I saw that my two greatest regrets when I died would be every moment which I had wasted not doing anything of value in the eyes of God, and all of the time and energy which I had wasted worrying about not being loved when every moment of my existence I was bathed in an infinite sea of love, although unaware of it. [10]

Olivia and I had also walked Cape Cod's marshes and woods. There we had spoken of God. She had been spiritually desolate too, and I had been unable to help her.

In the chapel I rose from my knees. I kissed Olivia's forehead in the casket, then exited the chapel for the main sanctuary, where we would soon pray the Rosary.

Olivia had not had Roy's experience of infinite love on the

Cape. But I believed she had had it in the hotel room where she died. There Jesus had come to her, revealed His love for her, and led her home to the Father.

9

FUNERAL

Upon the altar in St. Matthew's main sanctuary, six priests were concelebrating a funeral Mass for Olivia.

Father Reid had come from his parish of St. Ann to preside. Joining him were Fathers John Allen from St. Matthew; Benjamin Roberts from Our Lady of Lourdes; Joshua Voitus from my former parish of St. Vincent; Dennis Kuhn from Holy Angels; and Abbot Placid Solari from Belmont Abbey, who, at Bob Gallagher's request, had offered Mass for Olivia the day after she died.

I remembered a comment a priest-friend had made to me. In life, he remarked, the Church treats her children as humble servants. But when they die, everyone is buried a king or queen.

I had found this true myself and was grateful for it. The world lauds the strong and forgets them when they falter. In contrast, the Church finds its treasures in the poor, sick, and weak. Their sufferings conform them to Jesus, and open them to loving and being loved.

Like George Bailey in *It's a Wonderful Life*, Olivia's depression hid from her the many lives she touched. In death her influence was made plain. Her funeral was being held in one of the country's largest parishes, with six priests on the altar. Family had rushed from New England, Virginia, Florida and Australia to say goodbye.

Before Mass started I had come in from the chapel and taken my seat next to Melanie. The congregation had prayed a Rosary for Olivia. Then Tim delivered a eulogy that beautifully captured Olivia's compassion and thoughtfulness. He spoke of their time together at East Carolina University, and how Olivia looked out for him, both while they were students together and after she graduated:

> Whenever I needed comfort and support, no matter what she was doing, Olivia would hop in her car or catch a plane to come and see me. Even when her flight was rerouted to Virginia, or she took a wrong turn and ended up in, yup, you guessed it, Virginia, she didn't mind, she was just happy that she was able to take care of, and spend time with, her little brother. As a big sister, Olivia was unmatched. Even when it was most inconvenient for her, she was there when I needed her.

Olivia, said Tim, was a nurturer. This found expression in her first job after college, as a teaching assistant at St. Ann's Catholic

School in Charlotte. Her students recognized it. They even, said Tim, "went as far as to invite her to sit with them at lunch...an honor that is not given lightly."

Above all, it was at Holy Angels where Olivia truly thrived.

Olivia hugging Tim

Olivia, said Tim, cared deeply for the residents of Holy Angels, and through her selflessness and compassion provided them with a sense of acceptance and peace.

> Whether it be her family, friends, or the people she cared for, Olivia brought joy to all those around her. Her smile could light up a room, her laughter was contagious, and while outwardly

beautiful, her true beauty lay in her desire to better the lives of others.

The name "Olivia" means "gift of peace." I can't think of a name more fitting, as being in her presence brought about a profound sense of calm and relaxation that only she could provide...Life is filled with uncertainty. However, there is one thing that I am 100% sure of, and that is that the world would be a better place if everyone could be, even just a little bit more, like Olivia.

After Tim's eulogy Olivia's funeral Mass began. In Scripture and song, we gave praise for Christ's victory over sin and death. The second reading especially spoke to me. I had chosen the passage, from chapter 8 of Saint Paul's Letter to the Romans, and been honored when Conor read it, ascending to the ambo while three of his sons, Peter, Jude and Paul, served by the altar:

> *What will separate us from the love of Christ? Will anguish, or distress, or persecution, or famine, or nakedness, or peril, or the sword?...No, in all these things we conquer overwhelmingly through him who loved us. For I am convinced that neither death, nor life, nor angels, nor principalities, nor present things, nor future things, nor powers, nor height, nor depth, nor any other creature will be able to separate us from the love of God in Christ Jesus our Lord.*

In the *Diary* Jesus speaks of "My omnipotent mercy." Saint Faustina deepens our understanding of this mystery, but she is not the first to reveal it. It is a Biblical truth, beautifully set forth in these verses from Saint Paul. Nothing but our own final and definitive rejection of Him can separate us from Christ, who has given everything for us. His mercy is greater than our anguish. His love is stronger than death.

Up on the altar, Father Reid prayed the words of consecration:

> *Take this, all of you, and eat of it: For this is My Body which will be given up for you.*

In a moment we would receive Him, life of our souls.

As I prepared I remembered an insight Bishop Curlin had received from Mother Teresa, and which he in turn had shared with me. "Jesus brings all Heaven with Him in Holy Communion," the great saint of Calcutta had told him. "You can't separate Jesus from Heaven."

Father Reid concluded the Communion Rite. Jesus was truly present, though veiled under the appearance of bread. Father Reid held Him before us that we might adore Him:

> *Behold the Lamb of God, behold Him who takes away the sins of the world. Blessed are those called to the supper of the Lamb.*

With the congregation Melanie and I confessed our

unworthiness to receive Him. Then we rose and entered the line for Holy Communion.

In a few moments, for a few moments, we would be at the supper of the Lamb. Olivia would be there too.

The funeral had been beautiful, *one part sorrow, two parts joy*. The joy was in Christ's presence, the assurance of His victory, the music, prayers, and blessings, and in the closeness of family and friends.

Now, as we recessed, came the sorrow.

Olivia was the first congregant to leave from the church, not wearing a wedding dress, not hand in hand with a groom, but in a casket. Melanie and I slid into our car and joined the funeral procession to Forest Lawn Cemetery East, across from Heritage Funeral Home.

The number of mourners at the cemetery was smaller and more somber. Father Reid led us in a few final prayers. Then, during the Hour of Mercy, we laid Olivia to rest.

As Melanie and I returned to our car we walked with James Hetzel. Twenty-four years earlier, James had brought my young family to Charlotte to take a position in an exciting start-up that would become The Catholic Company. We had stayed in his house. James' wonderful wife Whitney had watched Olivia with her own children, four at the time, later to become nine. We had seen each other's families grow.

James smiled sadly. "I'm so sorry Rick." His smile seemed to acknowledge that even with the real consolations of faith, this life is still a vale of tears.

Like Bob and Conor, James assured me I was a good father. All three men knew how easily I could let myself be haunted by *what-ifs* and regrets.

I thanked James. We separated and went back to our cars.

Melanie and I headed towards Paradiso. Friends and family would be coming over soon, to share memories of Olivia over a meal of pasta, meatballs and sausage.

As we drove I was jolted by a thought.

"Darling, do you remember the dream you had before Olivia died, of riding in a car with my Mum and Dad? We thought it might be a funeral. In the dream an old man and a young man involved in Catholic publishing had said some kind things about me, and you were recounting these to my parents. Do you remember?"

"Yes, of course," said Melanie. The dream and our conversation about it the following morning had left a strong impression.

"Do you think the dream could have been God preparing us for Olivia's death? And the two men; could they have been Bob and Conor? As if God were communicating in advance, *take their words to heart. It wasn't your fault. You were a good father, Rick.*"

Melanie looked at me, her eyes widening. She squeezed my hand.

"Yes. Yes, I do," she said. "I believe that was God was preparing you for Olivia."

We continued, my heart marveling at the mercy of God. In a single swoop, he had freed me of any burden of self-recrimination I might have carried for Olivia — as easily and definitively as Robert De Niro's character was freed of his penitential ballast in the movie *The Mission*.

Melanie and I arrived home and pulled up the long driveway of Paradiso. A few of our family had beaten us there. A dear friend had retrieved our trays of food from our go-to Italian caterer and set them up inside.

As friends and family arrived and ate and laughed for the next few hours, the ache of missing Olivia was quieted. It was a blessing to remember humorous and endearing stories of Olivia with my parents and family, who had known Olivia since she was born. And it was a blessing to catch up, too, on the lives of friends and cousins who had come, whom I saw rarely and loved.

Funerals and their attendant ceremonies are times not only of farewell but of coming together. One of the cherished stories in the Rotondi family is how my Uncle Arthur and Aunt Karen began their courtship at a wake.

As the evening progressed our guests dwindled. Soon all who remained with Melanie and me were Tim and Elizabeth and a few close friends.

Tim called for attention. "I'd like to make an announcement," he said, beaming. Elizabeth was beaming too.

"Olivia's death has been hard, but Elizabeth has been here for me every step of the way." Tim and Elizabeth looked at each other with love. "Elizabeth, you've been my rock, and you are the woman I'm going to marry!"

We applauded and cheered. It wasn't the formal engagement yet. That would come eight months later, when Tim presented

Elizabeth with a beautiful diamond ring, the phrase *You are my rock* inscribed on the inner band.

It was however a mutual affirmation of their intent to marry and a sharing of that intent with us. Their love and generosity had been tested by tragedy and become even stronger and more beautiful. They would marry on October 7, Feast of the Holy Rosary, in 2023.

That night, when we had turned in and were about to go to sleep, I told Melanie how grateful I was for her being my rock through the bereavement. I was grateful for her love, and for the new people she had given me to love, her children and grandchildren — now my grandchildren, too.

I kept my one regret to myself: that Olivia had gone with our relationship to some degree strained, that she hadn't addressed me on her suicide note, that we never had a proper goodbye.

10

CHARLESTON

On May 12, the day after we buried Olivia, Melanie and I embarked on the three-and-a-half-hour drive to Charleston to attend the Episcopal Ordination of Bishop-elect Jacques Fabre-Jeune the next day.

Melanie received an emailed invitation on May 4, which we accepted immediately. One hundred and fifty years ago Melanie's maternal ancestors, immigrants from Ireland, were among the relative handful of South Carolinian Catholics. They were faithful parishioners of an historic parish in Columbia, the Basilica of Saint Peter, for generations. They praised God as both their parish and the Diocese of Charleston took root and flourished. Now we would be present as our new bishop was installed at the Charleston Convention Center in front of thousands.

The invitations to the Episcopal Ordination seemed serendipitous for several reasons. For one thing, we didn't think we deserved them. We loved our diocese and were active with the Rock Hill Oratory. We weren't as active with the diocese and didn't receive many diocesan communications. Our contributing level was closer to the "widow's mite" than the "major donor" end of the scale.

The invitation arrived as a surprise and unmerited gift fewer than 10 days before the event. Further, the bishop's Episcopal Ordination on May 13 coincided with the one-year anniversary of my marriage proposal and Melanie's wonderful "yes!" Attending would be a way for us to affirm our own vocational commitment — and to tack on a celebratory day or two along the South Carolina Coast after.

"Are you sure you still want to go, darling?" Melanie asked me before we left Paradiso.

"Yes, I am," I replied. We had prayed for Olivia and buried her and laughed and cried with family and friends who had come to help us mourn. We would grieve her for months and miss her forever. But it was important for me and Melanie to have this time now.

In the afternoon we pulled into the TravelSuites across from the Convention Center. After settling in, we looked again at the schedule of events. The Episcopal Ordination was tomorrow afternoon. This evening at 6 p.m. there was a Vespers service at the Cathedral of St. John the Baptist in downtown Charleston. We looked at the clock doubtfully. Though we didn't have much time, we decided to go.

We headed to the Cathedral on Charleston's famous Broad Street and found parking in the back. We were running late. We walked quickly to the front of the Cathedral, passing a side yard with a large tent and staff setting up for a festive reception. Then we went in.

The Cathedral was beautiful. The Diocese of Charleston was established in 1820. It is one of the oldest dioceses in the country, the august ecclesiastical mother of the dioceses of Savannah, Raleigh, Atlanta, and Charlotte. The arches and statues and stained glass of the Cathedral, the reverence of the servers, the splendor of the vestments, and the angelic harmony of the choirs were the fruit of 200 years of the faith being planted at this spot. Melanie and I sat rapt through the service and the homily of Bishop-elect Jacques. We recessed to the ethereal stanzas of the *Salve Regina*.

We left the Cathedral and headed back to our car. An usher stopped us.

"This way to the reception," he told us. I was excited and surprised. I hadn't realized our invitations included the reception too, an event that looked like it was for a few hundred people at most.

We turned the corner of the Cathedral and headed to the tented area we had passed coming in. As we did, we almost ran into Bishop-elect Jacques. He was alone and heading into a side door, presumably to change his vestments before the reception in his honor. We were all surprised and a little amused by the near collision. Bishop-elect Jacques flashed his big smile and directed us to the reception he would soon join.

"That was odd!" Melanie said.

The reception for Bishop-elect Jacques was amazing. The charcuterie boards, placed generously throughout the reception area, offered the most exquisite assortment of meats and cheeses and crudités we had ever seen. The dinner courses, piled high on silver platters, included dishes from Bishop-elect Jacques' native Haiti mixed with traditional Charlestonian fare. Melanie and I feasted on Cuban chicken, grilled pineapple and plantains, and tender roast beef, concluding our meal with miniature Key lime pies.

Melanie and I mingled with the other guests, the close friends and collaborators of Bishop-elect Jacques, for almost two hours. We connected with a dear Facebook friend, Sister Margaret Kerry with the Daughters of St. Paul, and learned more about the history of Charleston from some of its most learned and active lay Catholics. We chatted with retiring Bishop Gugliamone and Archbishop Hartmayer of Atlanta. Melanie was able to recommend to Archbishop Hartmayer one of her favorite books, *Catholicity in the Carolinas and Georgia*, a detailed history of the establishment and growth of the Church in the region published in 1879. The book was authored by Father Jeremiah Joseph O'Connell, a prominent one-time pastor of Melanie's family parish, the Basilica of Saint Peter. Father O'Connell would later go on to help found Belmont Abbey near Charlotte.

During the reception I scanned our program for the pictures and bios of the over one dozen bishops who would attend Bishop-elect Jacques' ordination to the episcopacy the next day.

"Is that the Papal Nuncio?" I asked Melanie and a few guests with whom we were chatting. I nodded towards a cleric with a confident demeanor and a crisp black cassock with purple sash.

One of the guests laughed. "That's our pastor, Father Gary Linsky!" Father Linsky, it turned out, was rector of none other than the Basilica of Saint Peter. Melanie and our new friends were delighted by my misidentification, as was Father Linsky when he learned of it. It became a source of merriment and gentle ribbing throughout the evening.

The most laughter, however, was prompted by an exchange with Bishop-elect Jacques, who graciously received and posed for photographs with all his guests.

Rick with Bishop Jacques Fabre-Jeune

As Melanie and I approached, he drew us in close. He draped his arms over our shoulders, one on each side, as we faced the camera.

"Now I am Jesus, right? I am Jesus."

Melanie and I tentatively agreed. Ordination empowers all priests to act *in persona Christi* when they confect the Sacraments. Bishops receive this power in its fullness, as only they can ordain other priests. In a real sense, episcopal ordination configures bishops to Christ more closely than everyone else on earth.

"You know what that means?" Bishop-elect Jacques continued.

We shook our heads quizzically.

"It means I am between two thieves!"

We all laughed. I reflexively added, "I am the good thief!" Melanie protested good-naturedly, and Bishop-elect Jacques looked skeptical. "I don't know about that!" he said.

Three hours after we arrived for Vespers, Melanie and I headed back to the TravelSuites, happy and at peace. It seemed impossible to be so one day after burying Olivia. But we were. We had worshipped and listened to heavenly music in Charleston's beautiful cathedral. We had been invited to a banquet as festive and enchanting as anything out of Narnia or Camelot. We had enjoyed fellowship and conversation with wonderful people. And we had, we felt, been hugged by Jesus, in the person of Bishop-elect Jacques. That all this was unplanned, unanticipated, and so incongruous with the past week's events made it seem like a special providence.

The next day, May 13, Melanie and I drove across the street from the TravelSuites to the Charleston Convention Center for the Episcopal Ordination. As I had done in proposing to Melanie, Bishop Jacques had chosen this date in honor of Our Lady of Fatima, whose feast day it was. As a young boy in Haiti he had fallen deathly ill. His mother had taken him to a church, knelt before a statue of Mary, and implored, *Please, Blessed Mother, obtain the healing of my son, and I will consecrate him to you*.

Now here he was, a bishop-elect, a successor to the Apostles, about to be installed on Mary's feast day.

As we neared the Convention Center, Melanie poured over Google Maps for an entryway that would protect us from the rain. Everyone else was parking in the lot in front of the Center and dashing through the main doors. Melanie found an alternate route. It allowed us to access the Center through an empty parking garage, entering on the little-used second floor and then descending to the main hall on the bottom level.

The Episcopal Ordination of Bishop Jacques Fabre-Jeune May 13, 2022

As we entered the Center, walking the seemingly abandoned hallway, Melanie and I once again almost ran into Bishop-elect Jacques. The second level was being used as a sacristy and vesting area. We nodded quick greetings and continued on our way.

Melanie squeezed my hand. "That's the second time in less than twenty-four hours we've unexpectedly come face-to-face with Bishop-elect Jacques!" I marveled too. It seemed more than coincidence. It seemed, again, like a hug from the Lord, a sign of His presence and care.

The Episcopal Ordination itself was extraordinary. Bishop Jacques was consecrated by Cardinal Wilton Gregory of Washington, D.C., together with Archbishop John Hartmayer of Atlanta and Bishop Luis Zarama of Raleigh. Concelebrators of the Mass included Archbishop Christophe Pierre (the actual Papal Nuncio to the United States, whom I had been scanning for at the Vespers reception) and nine additional bishops.

Joyful congregants filled the Convention Center with prayer and song. They were white, black, and Hispanic and had come from Charleston and South Carolina and other parishes and communities where Bishop Jacques had ministered and lived. The presence of the Holy Spirit was palpable.

Melanie and I entered the Center and settled into seats far in the back. Before Mass started, we walked about, nodding to friends and enjoying the profound beauty of the moment. During our meanderings we came upon friends from the Oratory with seats a few rows from the front — including two extras they generously offered to us. Melanie and I watched this historic act of the Church with awe from about 60 feet away.

As we did so, I was struck by the universality and fruitfulness of the Church. I had been pierced by this vision at the General Audience with Pope Francis in Rome in 2016. Seeing in the gathered faithful the fulfillment of Biblical promises, such as that the Lord will build an everlasting Temple and be a light to the nations, had prompted me to create *Messiah*. Now I had this experience again. I saw in the Episcopal Ordination of Bishop Jacques the Lord making all things new, enriching

His Church with fresh gifts and cultures and people while preserving its existing treasures and beauties (Mt 13:52). I saw the mustard seed that had been planted in Charleston 200 years ago bearing fruit 100-fold.

After Mass and the installation ceremony, we exited the Center. Melanie and I lingered for a moment, chatting with some priests of the diocese and waiting for the bishops to process through.

Melanie mentioned to one of the priests her association with the Basilica of Saint Peter, an association she shared not only with Fathers Jeremiah Joseph O'Connell and Gary Linsky but with the late Cardinal Joseph Bernardin, who had grown up in the parish. Cardinal Bernardin had ordained Cardinal Gregory to the episcopacy, just as Cardinal Gregory had ordained Bishop Jacques today.

"Would you like to meet the Cardinal?" said the priest unexpectedly. "Come up here and see if you can greet him." As Cardinal Gregory approached, Melanie called out, "I love Cardinal Bernardin, too! I grew up in his home parish." Cardinal Gregory paused and beamed, "He's the reason I wear this!" he said, pointing to his pectoral cross.

Melanie and I headed to the doors of the Center, feeling happy and incredibly blessed.

Once again we were stopped by an usher. "This way to the reception." And once again, we found ourselves banqueted by the bishop, celebrating and fellowshipping with his friends and chancery staff.

In the early evening, we said goodbye to our new friends and left the Convention Center and Charleston for Myrtle Beach.

It was a two-and-a-half-hour drive along the South Carolina coast. Melanie and I would be spending the weekend at Palm Ocean Villas, our beloved, no-frills timeshare located right on the Grand Strand.

Melanie at Myrtle Beach, SC

During the ride we excitedly discussed the extraordinary consolations we had received in Charleston. These continued during the remainder of our trip to Myrtle Beach. In addition to the natural and healing consolations of sun, views, waves, and sand, which we were blessed to receive often from Palm Ocean Villas, two unusual moments stood out.

One was at Gardenia's, a restaurant with a breakfast buffet that was a long-time favorite of Melanie's family. We enjoyed breakfast there on this trip as well. For the first time in Melanie's experience, we were told our meal was already taken care of when we approached the counter to pay. A friendly couple waved to us.

"We had two extra vouchers from our hotel and decided to pay for you," they told us. We thanked them, moved by their thoughtful gift.

The second moment involved another meal. Melanie and I hoped to eat at Starfish Cafe, an ocean front restaurant near Palm Ocean Villas. The hostess was doubtful of her ability to seat us when we called for a Saturday night reservation, finally promising us a table somewhere if we arrived after 8 p.m. We decided to try our luck instead at 6 p.m., after attending the Saturday vigil Mass at nearby St. Andrew parish. We were led immediately to one of the best tables in the house.

In those few days in Charleston and Myrtle Beach, Melanie and I experienced what we both perceived as an embrace of the Lord. In a mysterious way, we believe it was an embrace from Olivia too.

C.S. Lewis had a similar experience after losing his close friend Charles Wiliams. "[It was] as if he had ceased to meet us in particular places in order to meet us everywhere," said Lewis. He described the experience as "vital and bracing...even, however the word may be misunderstood and derided, exciting."[11]

Lewis later elaborated on his experience in a letter to his friend Sheldon Vanauken, author of the spiritual memoir *A Severe Mercy*. As a college student, I had devoured *A Severe Mercy* and was fortunate enough to spend an afternoon with

Vanauken at his home. *The New Oxford Review* picked up a short piece I wrote about the visit — my first-published work.

Lewis' words to Vanauken, as recorded in *A Severe Mercy*, came back to me now, over 30 years later, with a special weight.

> "It is remarkable (I have experienced it), that sense that the dead person *is*. And also, I have felt, is active: can sometimes do more for you now than before – as if God gave them, as a kind of birthday present on arrival, some great blessing to the beloved they have left behind.[12]

During the days of our Charleston trip, I believe, through a gift of the Lord, I met Olivia everywhere.

The unexpected banquets and meals were expressions of love and the healing of a relationship that still bore strains when she died. They were the *Goodbye, I love you!* we never had on earth and her *I made it, Dad!* from the Father's home.

The hug from Bishop Jacques was somehow a hug from Olivia also, the goodbye hug her suicide had prevented, and which, through God's mercy, she offered now.

Above all, the Masses were moments of profound communion. As Mother Teresa said, we cannot separate Jesus from Heaven. *You cannot receive Jesus without receiving all Heaven too*.

For the rest of my life, in every Holy Communion, I would join Olivia, together with my fellow communicants, and all the angels and saints, in loving and being loved.

Epilogue

Stories of encountering deceased loved ones are not rare in the life of the Church. The testimonies of the apostles of their encounters with the Risen Lord are the heart of the Gospel. Jesus is the resurrection and the life (Jn 11:25), and He promises His followers they will share in His resurrection too.

Many saints have written of their experiences with departed family and friends. In her book *Heaven's Splendor and the Riches that Await You There*, Sister Mary Ann Fatula, OP gives an overview of several accounts.

Saint Gregory of Nazianzus felt the constant assistance and guidance of his deceased friend, Saint Basil. Saint Ambrose of Milan said of his deceased brother, Satyrus, "you remain with me, and ever will remain." Saint Catherine of Siena experienced the love and protection of her deceased father, as did Saint Thérèse of Lisieux.[13]

Ordinary faithful have their stories too. These include encountering deceased loved ones in dreams; feeling assisted in practical matters, such as buying or selling a house or finding a job; or experiencing their closeness in natural phenomena and even the timely playing of radio songs.

The presence of cardinals (in the avian rather than ecclesial sense) is one natural phenomenon often connected with visits from the deceased. So common is the association that one of the largest grief support organizations in the Catholic Church, Red Bird Ministries, references it in its name.

When Olivia died I knew nothing of this. Cardinals, native to North and South America, are not mentioned in the Bible. I had never read about cardinal visits in the lives of the saints.

Yet in the days after Olivia died, I began to notice cardinals at Paradiso. Melanie and I had not been aware of them before. Of course they may have been here, and probably were. Now, however, they were attracting our attention, commanding our notice when we had no reason to look.

Cardinal seen at the NC Zoo, May 2022

Three weeks after Olivia died, Melanie and I took our grandchildren, Jaxon, age 9, and Penny, age 4, to the North Carolina Zoo in Asheboro. I had taken Olivia and Tim here several times before, including when Olivia was nearly the same age as Penny.

Like Olivia, Penny had long brown hair, brown eyes, and a sweet affectionate nature. When Penny held my hand or asked me to carry her, memories of Olivia came flooding back.

The memories were heartbreaking and wonderful at the same time: *one part sorrow, two parts joy*.

At the zoo I noticed a cardinal following us. Its behavior was striking, so much so that of the five pictures I took that day, four were of the cardinal.

I didn't know why I was having these cardinal encounters. Google provided answers, showing me the connection with deceased loved ones. I became more sensitive to the timing of these appearances. They seemed to coincide with occasions that Olivia might find special or significant. I came to believe that behind the scenes, Olivia was sending cardinals to encourage me — as Flor, in the movie *Spanglish*, sends the family dog Chum to console her employer when she cannot be present herself.

Others, including my mother, my sister, Emily, and some of Olivia's friends, spoke of experiencing Olivia's presence through butterflies. They told us of beautiful butterflies fluttering, lingering, tracing embraces in the air, appearing alone and out of season, or outside their typical range.

The butterfly accounts sent chills down our spines. At Paradiso, our lantana bushes and open pastureland attract troupes of butterflies every year. We didn't notice a change with

Olivia's passing. With cardinals, however, we did. We put up a few bird feeders to encourage them to stay. We grew accustomed to seeing one or two every morning as we drank our coffees on our front porch, a near-daily reminder of Olivia.

The morning of my 54th birthday, not quite four months after Olivia died, Melanie called me to join her on the porch.

"Darling, come quick, you have to see this!" About a dozen cardinals were visiting our bird feeder. There were three or four times as many cardinals feeding, flapping and preening as we had ever seen at one time.

On the vigil of my 55th birthday, Melanie and I reminisced about the extraordinary cardinal visit a year earlier. "I don't expect them back," I said to Melanie. "I don't think God works that way."

Rainbow over Paradiso August 27, 2023

About a half hour later, a light rain began to fall. Soon a beautiful rainbow stretched across the sky, nearly identical to the one that had appeared the day after Olivia died.

Natural phenomena such as cardinals, butterflies, and

rainbows were not our only connections to Olivia. Tim, my father, and my cousin Ellen all reported vivid dreams of Olivia, in which she communicated her well-being and assured them of her love.

Deacon Ed Kelly from Divine Saviour parish pulled me aside one Sunday after Mass. He offered condolences for Olivia and said he was praying *to* her. "We have a new intercessor up there," said Deacon Ed with an upward glance. "Let's put her to work!"

Residents and staff at Holy Angels felt they had an intercessor in Olivia too. Father Dennis displayed Olivia's photo in his chapel. "I feel closer to her now than ever before," he wrote me.

When the daughter of a friend generously proposed building a memorial garden for Olivia at Holy Angels as a service project, Father Dennis gratefully accepted. Shortly before the one-year anniversary of Olivia's death, about 20 friends and family gathered in front of "Olivia's Garden" in front of one of the resident homes to place a beautiful angel statue there. Residents whom Olivia had fed, washed, and cared for came outside to connect with her again.

Everything I kept for myself is lost; everything I gave away is mine forever. Bishop Curlin taught me these dying words of his mentor, Auxiliary Bishop John McNamara of Washington, DC. They were words Bishop Curlin himself lived by, too.

I saw their truth with Olivia. Her legacy was her works of mercy, the care she gave the residents at Holy Angels. They are a crown that will not fade or tarnish, one that she will wear in Heaven forever.

Olivia's Memorial Garden at Holy Angels

As time passes, I've felt most connected with Olivia when I see more clearly how closely her life is intertwined with Divine Mercy. Two such experiences stand out.

The first happened on the one-year anniversary of Olivia's death. Melanie and I had asked for a Mass to be said for Olivia at Divine Saviour. When we arrived Father Adilso had been called away. Deacon Ed would lead a Communion service instead.

Melanie and I participated in the Communion service. Despite myself, I was a little disappointed by the loss of the anniversary Mass.

During Deacon Ed's homily I was struck by a seemingly off-hand comment.

"Did you hear what Deacon Ed said?" I asked Melanie excitedly as we exited the church. "I think he said today is the anniversary of the establishment of the Feast of Divine Mercy!"

We did a quick search on our phones. It was true. The Church proclaimed the Feast of Divine Mercy on May 5, 2000 — 21 years to the day before Olivia died.

The second experience happened a few months later, in early July of 2023. Melanie and I were on a road trip to Wolfeboro, New Hampshire, to see family. We planned our route to allow a brief visit to the National Shrine of The Divine Mercy in Stockbridge, Massachusetts. We had visited the Shrine two years earlier, a celebratory visit as honeymooners, shortly after our wedding. Now we were visiting as mourners, a little over a year after Olivia's death.

The Candle Shrine

In the Our Lady of Mercy Candle Shrine, I lit candles for Olivia and other loved ones. In the adjacent Oratory, I knelt and thanked God for the extraordinary invitation to pray the Divine

Mercy Novena before Olivia died, and for the prompting Melanie and I received to confess and receive Holy Communion on Divine Mercy Sunday, placing the graces received in the hands of Our Lady.

"Would you like to go into the Gift Shop?" Melanie asked as we exited the Oratory.

"No, I don't think so," I said. We still had a long drive to Wolfeboro. As a Catholic publishing veteran, I figured I was already familiar with what was inside — though truthfully merchandising and presentations in well-run shops like the Shrine's change frequently. "I do need to make a quick visit to the restroom though."

Restrooms were located across from the Gift Shop. When I came out, for some reason, instead of leaving I went over to the Gift Shop to take a quick peek inside.

I opened the door, and was overwhelmed with cardinals: cardinal statues, cardinal ornaments, cardinal lapel pins, cardinal prints and cardinal tapestries. At this moment in time, July of 2023, the whole entry aisle seemed to be given over to cardinals, each one assuring me of Olivia's presence and encouragement.

It was like my birthday visit of the previous year, raised to a factor of ten. It was a message, not whispered as others had been, but shouted.

Olivia was enfolded in the most compassionate Heart of Jesus. Her life was a testimony to Divine Mercy. And she wanted, she wants, that testimony shared with others — that we might praise the omnipotence of the Divine Mercy forever.

"He will wipe away every tear from their eyes, and death shall be no more, neither shall there be mourning, nor crying, nor pain, for the former things have passed away."

— Revelation 21:4

ENDNOTES

1. As recorded by the medieval mystic Julian of Norwich in her spiritual classic, *Revelations of Divine Love.*

2. Saint Therese of Lisieux. Story of a Soul (l'Histoire d'une Ame): The Autobiography of St. Therese of Lisieux. CCEL online edition, excerpted from chapter 10. Retrieved here: https://ccel.org/ccel/therese/autobio/autobio.xviii.html

3. Saint Therese of Lisieux. Story of a Soul (l'Histoire d'une Ame): The Autobiography of St. Therese of Lisieux., cf this excerpt from Chapter 11, "Above all, I thirst for the Martyr's crown...I do not sigh for one torment; I need them all to slake my thirst." CCEL online edition. Retrieved here: https://ccel.org/ccel/therese/autobio/autobio.xix.html?

4. For this image, as in so much else, I am indebted to C.S. Lewis. "Then comes the sudden jab of red-hot memory and all this 'commonsense' vanishes like an ant in the mouth of a furnace." *A Grief Observed.* Original edition Faber & Faber. 1961.

5. Saint Augustine of Hippo, *The Confessions, B*ook VI, Chapter 13: New Advent web edition. Retrieved here: https://www.newadvent.org/fathers/110106.htm

6. Saint Augustine of Hippo, *The Confessions, B*ook III, Chapter 11. New Advent web edition. Retrieved here: https://www.newadvent.org/fathers/110103.htm

7. Tassone, Susan. *Praying with the Saints for the Holy Souls in Purgatory,* cf pages 71-72. Our Sunday Visitor. 2009.

8. Attributed to Saint Mother Teresa of Calcutta by multiple sources, including author Joseph Ranseth here: https://josephranseth.com/15-quotes-from-mother-teresa-to-cultivate-love-and-compassion/

9. Saint Maria Faustina Kowalska, *Diary of Saint Maria Faustina Kowalska: Divine Mercy in My Soul.* p. 524 - 527. Marian Press. 2000.

10. Schoeman, Roy. *Roy Schoeman's Conversion Story.* Reprinted online by Catholic Education Resource Center,https://www.catholiceducation.org/en/faith-and-character/faith-and-character/roy-schoeman-s-conversion-story.html

11. Lewis, C.S. (Ed.). From the Preface to *Essays Presented to Charles Williams.* Oxford University Press. 1947.

12. Vanauken, Sheldon. *A Severe Mercy*, quoting a personal letter to the author from C.S. Lewis, p. 184. Harper & Row. 1987. (Original work published 1977).

13. Fatula, Sister Mary Ann. *Heaven's Splendor: And the Riches that Await You There.* Sophia Institute Press. 2019.

HOW TO PRAY THE DIVINE MERCY CHAPLET

Praying the Divine Mercy Chaplet

1. Make the Sign of the Cross

In the name of the Father, and of the Son, and of the Holy Spirit. Amen.

2. Optional Opening Prayer

You expired, Jesus, but the source of life gushed forth for souls, and the ocean of mercy opened up for the whole world. O Fount of Life, unfathomable Divine Mercy, envelop the whole world and empty Yourself out upon us.

(Repeat three times)
O Blood and Water, which gushed forth from the Heart of Jesus as a fount of mercy for us, I trust in You!

3. Our Father

Our Father, Who art in Heaven, hallowed be Thy name; Thy kingdom come; Thy will be done on earth as it is in Heaven. Give us this day our daily bread; and forgive us our trespasses, as we forgive those who trespass against us; and lead us not into temptation, but deliver us from evil, Amen.

4. Hail Mary

Hail Mary, full of grace. The Lord is with thee. Blessed art thou amongst women, and blessed is the fruit of thy womb, Jesus.

Holy Mary, Mother of God, pray for us sinners, now and at the hour of our death, Amen.

5. The Apostles' Creed

I believe in God, the Father almighty, Creator of Heaven and earth, and in Jesus Christ, His only Son, our Lord, who was conceived by the Holy Spirit, born of the Virgin Mary, suffered under Pontius Pilate, was crucified, died and was buried; He descended into hell; on the third day He rose again from the dead; He ascended into Heaven, and is seated at the right hand of God the Father almighty; from there He will come to judge the living and the dead. I believe in the Holy Spirit, the holy Catholic Church, the Communion of Saints, the forgiveness of sins, the Resurrection of the body, and life everlasting. Amen.

6. The Eternal Father

Eternal Father, I offer You the Body and Blood, Soul and Divinity of Your Dearly Beloved Son, Our Lord, Jesus Christ, in atonement for our sins and those of the whole world.

7. On the 10 Small Beads of Each Decade

For the sake of His sorrowful Passion, have mercy on us and on the whole world.

8. Repeat for the remaining decades

Saying the "Eternal Father" (6) on the "Our Father" bead and then 10 "For the sake of His sorrowful Passion" (7) on the following "Hail Mary" beads.

9. Conclude with Holy God (Repeat three times)

Holy God, Holy Mighty One, Holy Immortal One, have mercy on us and on the whole world.

10. Optional Closing Prayer

Eternal God, in Whom mercy is endless and the treasury of compassion — inexhaustible, look kindly upon us and increase Your mercy in us, that in difficult moments we might not despair nor become despondent, but with great confidence submit ourselves to Your holy will, which is Love and Mercy itself.

HOW TO PRAY THE DIVINE MERCY NOVENA

A novena is typically nine days of prayer in preparation of a celebration of a feast day. At the National Shrine of The Divine Mercy, the Chaplet of Divine Mercy Novena is recited perpetually at the Hour of Great Mercy — the three o'clock hour.

The Chaplet can be said anytime, but the Lord specifically asked that it be recited as a novena. He promised, "By this Novena (of Chaplets), I will grant every possible grace to souls."

Intentions

For each of the nine days, our Lord gave Saint Faustina a different intention:

All mankind, especially sinners; the souls of priests and religious; all devout and faithful souls; those who do not believe in God and those who do not yet know Jesus; the souls who have separated themselves from the Church; the meek and humble souls and the souls of little children; the souls who especially venerate and glorify His mercy; the souls detained in purgatory; and souls who have become lukewarm.

"I desire that during these nine days you bring souls to the fountain of My mercy, that they may draw therefrom strength and refreshment and whatever grace they have need of in the hardships of life, and especially at the hour of death" (Diary, 1209).

First Day:

Today bring to Me ALL MANKIND, ESPECIALLY ALL SINNERS, and immerse them in the ocean of My mercy. In this way you will console Me in the bitter grief into which the loss of souls plunges Me.

Most Merciful Jesus, whose very nature it is to have compassion on us and to forgive us, do not look upon our sins but upon our trust which we place in Your infinite goodness. Receive us all into the abode of Your Most Compassionate Heart, and never let us escape from It. We beg this of You by Your love which unites You to the Father and the Holy Spirit.

Eternal Father, turn Your merciful gaze upon all mankind and especially upon poor sinners, all enfolded in the Most Compassionate Heart of Jesus. For the sake of His sorrowful Passion show us Your mercy, that we may praise the omnipotence of Your mercy for ever and ever. Amen.

Second Day:

Today bring to Me THE SOULS OF PRIESTS AND RELIGIOUS, and immerse them in My unfathomable mercy. It was they who gave Me strength to endure My bitter Passion. Through them as through channels My mercy flows out upon mankind.

Most Merciful Jesus, from whom comes all that is good, increase Your grace in men and women consecrated to Your service,* that they may perform worthy works of mercy; and that all who see them may glorify the Father of Mercy who is in heaven.

Eternal Father, turn Your merciful gaze upon the company of chosen ones in Your vineyard—upon the souls of priests and religious; and endow them with the strength of Your blessing. For the love of the Heart of Your Son in which they are enfolded, impart to them Your power and light, that they may be able to guide others in the way of salvation and with one voice sing praise to Your boundless mercy for ages without end. Amen.

Third Day:

Today bring to Me ALL DEVOUT AND FAITHFUL SOULS, and immerse them in the ocean of My mercy. These souls brought Me consolation on the Way of the Cross. They were that drop of consolation in the midst of an ocean of bitterness.

Most Merciful Jesus, from the treasury of Your mercy, You impart Your graces in great abundance to each and all. Receive us into the abode of Your Most Compassionate Heart and never let us escape from It. We beg this grace of You by that most wonderous love for the heavenly Father with which Your Heart burns so fiercely.

Eternal Father, turn Your merciful gaze upon faithful souls, as upon the inheritance of Your Son. For the sake of His sorrowful Passion, grant them Your blessing and surround them with Your constant protection. Thus may they never fail in love or lose the treasure of the holy faith, but rather, with all the hosts of Angels and Saints, may they glorify Your boundless mercy for endless ages. Amen.

Fourth Day:

Today bring to Me The PAGANS AND THOSE WHO DO NOT YET KNOW ME. I was thinking also of them during My bitter Passion, and their future zeal comforted My Heart. Immerse them in the ocean of My mercy.

Most compassionate Jesus, You are the Light of the whole world. Receive into the abode of Your Most Compassionate Heart the souls of those who do not believe in God and of those who as yet do not know You. Let the rays of Your grace enlighten them that they, too, together with us, may extol Your wonderful mercy; and do not let them escape from the abode which is Your Most Compassionate Heart.

Eternal Father, turn Your merciful gaze upon the souls of those who do not believe in You, and of those who as yet do not know You, but who are enclosed in the Most Compassionate Heart of Jesus. Draw them to the light of the Gospel. These souls do not know what great happiness it is to love You. Grant that they, too, may extol the generosity of Your mercy for endless ages. Amen.

Fifth Day:

Today bring to Me THE SOULS OF THOSE WHO HAVE SEPARATED THEMSELVES FROM MY CHURCH,* and immerse them in the ocean of My mercy. During My bitter Passion they tore at My Body and Heart, that is, My Church. As they return to unity with the Church, My wounds heal and in this way they alleviate My Passion.

Most Merciful Jesus, Goodness Itself, You do not refuse light to those who seek it of You. Receive into the abode of Your Most Compassionate Heart the souls of those who have separated themselves from Your Church. Draw them by Your light into the unity of the Church, and do not let them escape from the abode of Your Most Compassionate Heart; but bring it about that they, too, come to glorify the generosity of Your mercy.

Eternal Father, turn Your merciful gaze upon the souls of those who have separated themselves from Your Son's Church, who have squandered Your blessings and misused Your graces by obstinately persisting in their errors. Do not look upon their errors, but upon the love of Your own Son and upon His bitter Passion, which He underwent for their sake, since they, too, are enclosed in His Most Compassionate Heart. Bring it about that they also may glorify Your great mercy for endless ages. Amen.

Sixth Day:

Today bring to Me THE MEEK AND HUMBLE SOULS AND THE SOULS OF LITTLE CHILDREN, and immerse them in My mercy. These souls most closely resemble My Heart. They strengthened Me during My bitter agony. I saw them as earthly Angels, who will keep vigil at My altars. I pour out upon them whole torrents of grace. Only the humble soul is capable of receiving My grace. I favor humble souls with My confidence.

Most Merciful Jesus, You yourself have said, "Learn from Me for I am meek and humble of heart." Receive into the abode of Your Most Compassionate Heart all meek and humble souls and the souls of little children. These souls send all heaven into ecstasy and they are the heavenly Father's favorites. They are a sweet-smelling bouquet before the throne of God; God Himself takes delight in their fragrance. These souls have a permanent abode in Your Most Compassionate Heart, O Jesus, and they unceasingly sing out a hymn of love and mercy.

Eternal Father, turn Your merciful gaze upon meek souls, upon humble souls, and upon little children who are enfolded in the abode which is the Most Compassionate Heart of Jesus. These souls bear the closest resemblance to Your Son. Their fragrance rises from the earth and reaches Your very throne. Father of mercy and of all goodness, I beg You by the love You bear these souls and by the delight You take in them: Bless the whole world, that all souls together may sing out the praises of Your mercy for endless ages. Amen.

Seventh Day:

Today bring to Me THE SOULS WHO ESPECIALLY VENERATE AND GLORIFY MY MERCY,* and immerse them in My mercy. These souls sorrowed most over my Passion and entered most deeply into My spirit. They are living images of My Compassionate Heart. These souls will shine with a special brightness in the next life. Not one of them will go into the fire of hell. I shall particularly defend each one of them at the hour of death.

Most Merciful Jesus, whose Heart is Love Itself, receive into the abode of Your Most Compassionate Heart the souls of those who particularly extol and venerate the greatness of Your mercy. These souls are mighty with the very power of God Himself. In the midst of all afflictions and adversities they go forward, confident of Your mercy; and united to You, O Jesus, they carry all mankind on their shoulders. These souls will not be judged severely, but Your mercy will embrace them as they depart from this life.

Eternal Father, turn Your merciful gaze upon the souls who glorify and venerate Your greatest attribute, that of Your fathomless mercy, and who are enclosed in the Most Compassionate Heart of Jesus. These souls are a living Gospel; their hands are full of deeds of mercy, and their hearts, overflowing with joy, sing a canticle of mercy to You, O Most High! I beg You O God:

Show them Your mercy according to the hope and trust they have placed in You. Let there be accomplished in them the promise of Jesus, who said to them that during their life, but especially at the hour of death, the souls who will venerate this fathomless mercy of His, He, Himself, will defend as His glory. Amen.

Eighth Day:

Today bring to Me THE SOULS WHO ARE DETAINED IN PURGATORY, and immerse them in the abyss of My mercy. Let the torrents of My Blood cool down their scorching flames. All these souls are greatly loved by Me. They are making retribution to My justice. It is in your power to bring them relief. Draw all the indulgences from the treasury of My Church and offer them on their behalf. Oh, if you only knew the torments they suffer, you would continually offer for them the alms of the spirit and pay off their debt to My justice.

Most Merciful Jesus, You Yourself have said that You desire mercy; so I bring into the abode of Your Most Compassionate Heart the souls in Purgatory, souls who are very dear to You, and yet, who must make retribution to Your justice. May the streams of Blood and Water which gushed forth from Your Heart put out the flames of Purgatory, that there, too, the power of Your mercy may be celebrated.

Eternal Father, turn Your merciful gaze upon the souls suffering in Purgatory, who are enfolded in the Most Compassionate Heart of Jesus. I beg You, by the sorrowful Passion of Jesus Your Son, and by all the bitterness with which His most sacred Soul was flooded: Manifest Your mercy to the souls who are under Your just scrutiny. Look upon them in no other way but only through the Wounds of Jesus, Your dearly beloved Son; for we firmly believe that there is no limit to Your goodness and compassion. Amen.

Ninth Day:

Today bring to Me SOULS WHO HAVE BECOME LUKEWARM,* and immerse them in the abyss of My mercy. These souls wound My Heart most painfully. My soul suffered the most dreadful loathing in the Garden of Olives because of lukewarm souls. They were the reason I cried out: 'Father, take this cup away from Me, if it be Your will.' For them, the last hope of salvation is to run to My mercy.

Most compassionate Jesus, You are Compassion Itself. I bring lukewarm souls into the abode of Your Most Compassionate Heart. In this fire of Your pure love, let these tepid souls, who, like corpses, filled You with such deep loathing, be once again set aflame. O Most Compassionate Jesus, exercise the omnipotence of Your mercy and draw them into the very ardor of Your love, and bestow upon them the gift of holy love, for nothing is beyond Your power.

Eternal Father, turn Your merciful gaze upon lukewarm souls who are nonetheless enfolded in the Most Compassionate Heart of Jesus. Father of Mercy, I beg You by the bitter Passion of Your Son and by His three-hour agony on the Cross: Let them, too, glorify the abyss of Your mercy. Amen.

About the Author

Rick and Melanie Rotondi at the National Shrine of The Divine Mercy, 6/27/2021

Rick Rotondi is an author, producer, and Catholic publishing veteran and the founder and CEO of Cenacle, which he runs with his wife, Melanie.

In addition to *Love is Stronger than Death*, he is the writer and executive producer of *Messiah*; co-writer of the docuseries and book *Queen of Heaven*, and author of *101 Surprising Facts About the Bible*.

Rick and Melanie live on their farm, Paradiso, in York, South Carolina.

www.ingramcontent.com/pod-product-compliance
Lightning Source LLC
Chambersburg PA
CBHW070110080526
44586CB00013B/1251